# Cookin' on the Mississippi

### GOURMET FRENCH AND ENGLISH
### RECIPES FROM LOUISIANA AND MISSISSIPPI PLANTATIONS
### AND PADDLE WHEELERS.

*by Bobby Potts*

*Photographs by Edward A. Minvielle*

*Sweet potatoes Canon Burnt cake*

Some of the plantation homes pictured in this book have restaurants or catered food services and a few have overnight accommodations. Consult Tourist Information Centers at state lines or local tourist bureaus for further information on accommodations and hours. A few houses are only open for group tours, but most are open daily. Refer to map on inside back cover for locations.

The food was prepared by the plantations, by the boat chefs, and by co-operating restaurants. It was arranged by Bobby Potts and photographed by Ed Minvielle. The various pictures of the homes and the outbuildings were taken by Ed Minvielle, Ken Miguez, and Bobby Potts. Food on the Steamer Natchez was photographed by Vince Palumbo.

Bobby Potts has written two cookbooks previously and has lived in New Orleans, at Burnside on the Old River Road, and in Baton Rouge, has traveled extensively throughout Louisiana and Mississippi and is well acquainted with the cooking of the diverse regions of these two states. She is a former Botany professor, a botanical artist and painter, and cooking has been a lifetime hobby.

Ed Minvielle has done architectural photography for various Louisiana architects and is also a portrait photographer. He is a member of the Professional Photographers of Louisiana. Ed is very familiar with French cooking because he lives in New Iberia in South Louisiana and is a true native Acadian.

Special thanks to Sara Lemon, Mary Roseman and Marguerite Genre for their invaluable assistance.

Published and Distributed by
© Express Publishing Co., Inc.
305 Decatur Street
New Orleans, LA 70130
PRINTED IN HONG KONG
for Terrell Publishing Co.
10880122
ISBN: 0-935031-02-2

Photograph by Fonville Winans

*Bobby Potts*

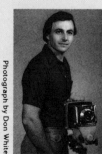

Photograph by Don White

*Ed Minvielle*

Cover Picture: Dining Room at Mt. Hope

Back Cover: Kitchen at Rosemont Plantation
(Recipes on page 43)
Food prepared by Ernesto Caldeira of Rosemont

# Cookin' on the Mississippi

Come with me to the Mighty Mississippi!

Come with me to savor cookin' on the Mississippi!

Come with me up the grand old mahogany and brass staircase of a paddlewheeler to the Texas Lounge and experience the wonders along the banks of the Mississippi River, in the world of "Delta Country."

You might prefer to take the Steamer Natchez or the Creole Queen or some of the many other "Queen" steamships to be found along the river or you may travel by car along the East or West River Roads and follow the paddle wheelers as they go. Whatever — your senses will be stimulated, your tastebuds tantalized, and your mind challenged to believe what your eyes see!

The waters that flow down together to produce the Mississippi bring with them top soil and minerals stolen from land in the North and this alluvial soil is deposited at the southern end of the river. Centuries ago this depositing started up in the middle of the South and flared outward to the Gulf of Mexico, forming a triangle of dark rich soil that produces some of the finest crops in the world. This is the Delta.

The wealthy Creoles came from France and Spain and purchased land in the lower Delta, while people of English descent, called "Les Americains" by the French, came from the east — Tennessee, North Carolina, Virginia and farther, to establish plantations in the upper Delta. Creoles — mostly French — were proud and sophisticated, a breed apart from the good peasant Acadians who migrated to Louisiana when expelled from French Canada, and conquered the swamps and marshes. The bond of French language was strong, however, and in time Creoles and Acadians intermarried and eventually almost completely absorbed the Spanish and German cultures of the area.

*The Creole Queen at the René Beauregard House in Chalmette*

Both French and English speaking planters built simple dwellings upon arrival, but crops of indigo, cotton, and later, sugar cane, produced such extreme wealth, that mansions of grand design began to appear rapidly on the flat lands of Louisiana and the rolling hills of Mississippi, in stark contrast to the small homes of their neighbors.

The enormous force of the river dominated the lives of plantation families, controlling transportation, location and architectural design of homes, the success of crops and marketing of produce — indeed, their entire life style. This richness of the soil produced an opulence that was unique. but carried with it much hard work by men and women alike during the antebellum (pre-Civil War) period. The plantation wife was often doctor, nurse, and welfare visitor to the workers on the plantation, and the master of the manor usually worked as hard as his overseer. The result was an abundance of creature comforts with an energy and zest for living that seized any occasion to hold soirees, masquerades, and all night balls. They entertained lavishly, set banquet boards with grand feasts of meats, seafoods and vegetables (often cooked in combination) and created the finest sauces and desserts imaginable.

Come let me introduce you to this wondrous collection of plantations — to this incredible, incredible river that has supported such varied and exciting cultures for more than two hundred years, to the romance of the paddle wheel boats, and to the cookin' of the Delta. *Cookin' on the Mississippi* is a collection of recipes for authentic foods of the French Creole and English American folks who lived and worked in these grand plantations, then and now.

Come aboard — we'll be rollin' on the river and Cookin' on the Mississippi!

*Destrehan Manor House*

# Destrehan Manor House
## Destrehan, Louisiana

*The first antebellum home we encounter on the tour up the Mississippi is Destrehan Manor House. One of Louisiana's very early homes, it was completed in 1790, with wings added about 1812. Having preceded the Grecian influence, it shows the high roof derived from homes of West Indies plantations and the typical arrangement of family rooms on the second level. Jean Noel d'Estrehan of Beaupré and his descendents occupied the house from 1802 to 1910, entertaining famous guests who ran the social gamut from Jean Lafitte, the pirate, to the Duc d'Orleans who later became King of France. The dining room presents an early brick mantle arranged with branches of Magnolia Grandiflora and a table set with an elegant cutwork tablecloth displaying fantastic French cuisine. The abundance of seafood in the Delta is evident in this menu planned by Royale Caterers of Kenner. The filets of trout topped with crabmeat sauce are accompanied by tomatoes stuffed with broccoli-rice, Shrimp Remoulade, stuffed artichokes with hollandaise sauce, crudités of raw cauliflower and carrots, and croissants with butter roses. A Croquembouche made of tiny cream puffs stacked upon each other, wound round with threads of caramelized sugar and adorned with candied violets and fresh strawberries, is the centerpiece of the buffet. (Croquembouche translates roughly into "mouth-munchie.")*

*Author's recipe*

# STUFFED ARTICHOKES with HOLLANDAISE SAUCE

Use six artichokes. Clip the barbs off the tips of the leaves and trim stems, if necessary, so they will sit upright. Boil in water seasoned with salt, red pepper and minced garlic. Drain upside down. Remove choke.

*Stuffing:*

| | |
|---|---|
| 1 cup grated Mozarella cheese | 1 teaspoon dried basil |
| 1 cup grated Parmesan cheese | 1 garlic clove, chopped |
| 2 cups herbed bread crumbs | or squeezed |
| 1 cup olive oil | 1 teaspoon rosemary |
| 2 tablespoons lemon juice | 1 tablespoon parsley |
| 6 Anchovy fillets, mashed into bits | Salt and pepper to taste |
| 6 slices of lemon | |

Combine all ingedients, but reserve 3/4 of the olive oil and the lemon slices. Pull leaves out gently with fingers and stuff mixture into each leaf. Pour the rest of the oil over the tops of the artichokes, letting it run down into leaves. Make a band of foil around each artichoke to secure the leaves. Place a lemon slice on top of each artichoke and place them upright in a covered baking dish with a little water in the bottom. Bake at 350° for 30 minutes or longer. Stuffing will get a little crust if you remove the lid near the end of baking time. These will freeze very well. Serve with hollandaise sauce and wedges of lemon.

# HOLLANDAISE SAUCE

Divide 1/4 pound butter into 3 pieces. Place 1 piece in top of double boiler with 2 egg yolks and 2 teaspoons lemon juice. Cook, stirring constantly, over hot, but not boiling water, gradually adding remaining butter. Cook, continuing to stir, about 2 minutes, or until as thick as desired. Remove from fire, add 1/4 teaspoon salt and a few grains of cayenne pepper. Continue beating for a few minutes. Add, if desired, 3 tablespoons of cream.

# TOMATOES STUFFED with BROCCOLI-RICE

Cut top off of six tomatoes and carefully scoop out inside. Place in a greased baking dish and fill with the broccoli-rice stuffing:

| | |
|---|---|
| 2 tablespoons butter | 1 cup cooked rice |
| 1 tablespoon chopped chives | 10 ounces frozen broccoli |
| 1 tablespoon chopped parsley | pieces (or fresh) |
| 1 teaspoon basil flakes | 1/2 cup sour cream |
| Salt and pepper to taste | 1/2 cup cheddar cheese |

Sauté chives, parsley and basil in butter till soft and light golden. Add cooked rice and broccoli bits (which have been cooked according to package directions) and toss lightly in the butter and herb mixture until well coated. Remove from heat and stir in sour cream. Fill tomatoes, top with cheddar cheese and bake in a preheated 350° oven for 20 minutes. A little water should be placed in the bottom of the baking dish. (If more tomato flavor is desired, chop up centers of tomatoes, cook down well and add to butter and herb mixture before adding rice.)

(See page 58 for Shrimp Remoulade and page 32 for Cream Puffs)

*Slave Cabin*

*Dining Room at Destrehan Manor House*

## FILETS OF TROUT with CRABMEAT SAUCE

Six-6 oz filets
1/2 cup shallots (green onions) chopped fine
1/2 cup milk
3 tablespoons flour
Salt & pepper to taste
One-8 oz carton of sour cream
1/2 stick of butter (margarine doesn't do as well in this recipe)
1 pound lump crabmeat

Sauté onions in butter until soft. Add flour and smooth into butter, but *do not brown*. Add milk, stirring and creaming continuously to prevent lumping. Add the sour cream and crab meat. Remove from heat. Brush filets with butter and place on a greased sheet pan or in a baking dish. Spoon an equal amount of the crabmeat sauce on each filet. Bake 30 minutes at 350°. Garnish with parsley, lemon and paprika. *Recipe from Shirlee Praetorius of Royale Caterers*

## PICKLED BEETS
(Picture on page 17)

1 can sliced beets, or small whole beets
Cider vinegar to cover beets
1/2 cup sugar
1 tablespoon finely chopped onion
1 teaspoon caraway seeds
1/4 teaspoon salt

Place all ingredients in pot with drained beets and bring to rapid boil. Remove from heat and allow to cool. Refrigerate.

4

# San Francisco Plantation
### Garyville, Louisiana

San Francisco is an architectural tribute to the ornate style of the riverboat. Valsin Marmillion incorporated the "Steamboat Gothic" image in his fantasy mansion and spent his last dollar to build it. According to early records, he orginally named his house "Sans Frusquin", an idiom that roughly means "without a red cent" which was corrupted by a later owner to the name San Francisco. A light meal for a summer evening is set in the Center Room, thus gathering the family from the surounding intricately decorated rooms into the quiet heart of the home. Gourmet Catering of La Place

*San Francisco Plantation House*

prepared Shrimp Armand which is served on a bed of saffron rice for the entrée. Hot oysters are served in patty shells and the supper is completed with avocado and shrimp salad, brussels sprouts in drawn butter, and Ambrosia — a favorite Louisiana dessert. The Creoles also loved to serve bubbling hot dark brown oyster stew in a "tureen-sized" patty shell called 'Vol-au-Vent', especially at Christmas time. Vol-au-Vent is the French term for our "Will-o'-the Wisp" and refers to the ethereal quality of the air-filled puff-pastry which must be served immediately.

## HOT OYSTERS in PATTY SHELLS

1 pint oysters, cut up with scissors
1 tablespoon butter or oleo
1 tablespoon flour
1 cup evaporated milk or cream
1 egg
Salt, pepper and cayenne to taste
Dash of nutmeg
1/4 cup chopped parsley
1 tablespoon Worcestershire sauce
2 tablespoons white wine

Melt butter, cream in flour and add half the cream and oyster liquor slowly over low heat. Beat egg with remaining milk and add gradually to white sauce. Put cut pieces of oysters in and add seasonings. Simmer 5 minutes and add Worcestershire sauce and wine. Serve in hot patty shells and garnish with a dollop of whip cream if you want to be fancy.

## SHRIMP ARMAND

1 pound cleaned shrimp - do not peel tip of tail
2 tablespoons butter (or more)
1 clove garlic
1 bell pepper, cut in large chunks
1 medium onion, cut in large chunks
Lemon juice, as you like
Worcestershire sauce, as you like
Water as needed
Salt and pepper to taste
Parsley

*Rain Cistern*

Melt butter, add juice of pressed garlic and some of the parsley which has been chopped fine. Toss chunks of pepper and onion lightly in butter. Add lemon juice and Worcestershire sauce while mixture simmers. Don't overcook. Add shrimp and seasoning just before vegetables are done. Cook 'till shrimp are pink and vegetables are just tender. Add water as needed to keep from scorching. Garnish with remaining parsley.

## SAFFRON RICE

Cook 2 cups long grain rice in large pot of boiling, salted water for 18 minutes. Drain, rinse and set colander over boiling water until rice is heated through again. Crush a half teaspoon saffron in 2 tablespoons hot water until well mashed and stirred. Add 3 tablespoons melted butter and mix into rice, along with salt and pepper. Serve at once, garnish with parsley.

## AVOCADO and SHRIMP SALAD

1 cup cooked, chopped shrimp
2 hard boiled eggs, chopped
1/2 cup finely chopped celery
1/4 cup finely chopped green onions
1/4 cup chopped parsley
1/2 cup chopped cucumber
2 tablespoons finely chopped
   bell pepper
4 tablespoons mayonnaise
2 teaspoons hot sweet mustard
Lemon - pepper and salt to taste

Toss all ingredients lightly but thoroughly. Pare two avocados and cut in half lengthwise. Remove seed, place halves on lettuce and fill with shrimp salad. Serve with fancy cut lemon or lemon wedge.

## AMBROSIA

1 dozen navel oranges
1 fresh coconut, save milk
1 bunch seedless green grapes
1 jar Maraschino cherries
1 cup miniature marshmallows
1 cup sour cream
1 cup sauterne
1/2 cup powdered sugar

Grate coconut. Peel oranges, slice, remove seeds and skin. Mix all ingredients together, including coconut milk. Let stand at least two hours, or preferably overnight in refrigerator. Serve with a cookie.

*Author's recipes*

5

# Oak Alley
## Vacherie, Louisiana

On the west bank of the Mississippi stands a magnificent home built in 1830 by Jacques Telesphore Roman, III, a former governor of Louisiana who named it Bon Sejour (Pleasant Sojourn). Since it was referred to by the crew of every passing riverboat as the "Oak Alley", that name has supplanted the first! Typical of plantation construction, the hand forged iron work and the kiln fired bricks were wrought by plantation labor. Boards in these homes were almost always of cypress though flooring was often of heart pine. We are treated to a luncheon on the front gallery, prepared by the plantation restaurant. Uncle Tobin's Creole Meatballs, cooked in the French tradition of the River Road Country, are very different from Italian meatballs. Theresa Harrison, a cook at the plantation who originated the recipe, served them so often at Uncle Tobin's request that they came to be named for him. We are also served a garden salad with buttermilk dressing, peas with pearl onions, pecan pie a-la-mode and of course — the ever present crusty loaves of French bread.

*Oak Alley Plantation House*

*Author's recipes*

## UNCLE TOBIN'S CREOLE MEAT BALLS

| | |
|---|---|
| 1-1/2 pounds ground round | 1/4 cup chopped parsley |
| 1 egg, slightly beaten | 1 small onion, chopped |
| 1/2 cup bread crumbs | 1 teaspoon basil |
| 1 teaspoon salt | 1 teaspoon thyme |
| Cayenne pepper to taste | 2 tablespoons salad oil |

Add egg and bread crumbs to meat and mix. Add all seasonings and mix thoroughly. Shape into balls with hands or meat baller. Keep water handy to rinse between each meatball. Fry until brown in salad oil. Drain and place in hot gravy made as follows:

| | |
|---|---|
| 2 tablespoons oil | 2 tablespoons lemon juice |
| 2 tablespoons flour | 1 teaspoon grated lemon peel |
| 1/4 cup green onions | Salt and cayenne pepper to taste |
| 1/4 cup chopped bell pepper | 1 can stewed tomatoes |
| 1/4 cup chopped celery | 1 can tomato sauce |
| 1/4 cup chopped parsley | 1/4 cup heavy, dark steak sauce |
| 1/2 cup mushrooms with liquor | 2 tablespoons sugar |
| 1/2 teaspoon finely chopped garlic | |

Make a roux with oil and flour. Add water gradually and all tomatoes. Mash tomatoes well. Let cook down and thicken. More water can be added later if needed. All vegetables and seasonings can be added raw or they can be sautéd first in a little bacon grease if you prefer. Add steak sauce and sugar last. Let meatballs simmer in gravy for about 1/2 hour or more for full flavor. Serve over spaghettini.

## METHOD FOR MAKING A ROUX

Use equal amounts of flour and shortening. Add flour to hot shortening, lower heat slightly and brown flour while constantly stirring and smoothing. The secret is to push the browning to the darkest degree possible without scorching the flour. It should become the color of chocolate. Turn heat very low before adding water, so grease doesn't flame up. Add water slowly and blend thoroughly each time until mixture has the consistency of a thin paste, then water may be added more rapidly in larger quantities. In the early stages of blending, it may be necessary to lift the pan from the heat or even remove it temporarily to keep roux creamy. It tends to lump when it is cooking faster than it can absorb the water.

## BUTTERMILK DRESSING

| | |
|---|---|
| 2 cups mayonnaise | 2 tablespoons Accent |
| 2 cups buttermilk | 1 tablespoon chopped onions |
| 1/2 teaspoon garlic powder | 1 tablespoon chopped parsley |
| Salt and pepper to taste | |

Mix thoroughly and refrigerate. This is better if it is allowed to stand a couple of days before using.

## GARDEN SALAD

Tear lettuce in chunks and fill a large shallow serving dish. Ring edge of bowl with tomato wedges. Cut fine shreds of carrot, red cabbage (and onion, if desired) and scatter generously over the top. Season to taste and pour buttermilk dressing over all.

## PERFECT PECAN PIE

| | |
|---|---|
| 5 egg yolks | 3 tablespoons margarine |
| 1 cup sugar | 1 cup broken pecan meats |
| 1 cup white Karo syrup | 5 egg whites, well beaten |
| Vanilla to taste | |

Cream margarine, sugar and egg yolks. Add syrup, vanilla and pecans and stir well. Fold in egg whites. Pour mixture into unbaked pastry shell and bake slowly at 325° for one hour until custard like in consistency. Serve with ice cream and a few pecans sprinkled over the top, or whipped cream. (See page 10 for pie crust.)

*Garconniere*

*Tezcuco Plantation House*

# Tezcuco Plantation
## Burnside, Louisiana

Almost in the shadow of the Sunshine Bridge the east bank of the Mississippi, a "raised cottage is hidden in a grove of Live Oak trees. That is ho Tezcuco was referred to in antebellum days, but k today's standards it is a small mansion with 15 for ceilings and some rooms that are 25 feet squar This strange name of Aztec origin was brought from a sojourn in Mexico by the builder, Benjam. Tureaud, another member of the Bringier family and refers to a place of rest. The interior plaste decorations on the ceilings are quite ornate and th side galleries are framed in cast iron trim of a grap vine design. A long table in the elegant dining room is filled with favorite foods of the area. Jeannett Daigle has fried bream (perch) freshly caught by her husband, and plump shrimp from the Gulf of Mexico She has added rice pilaf, the traditional mustard greens and corn on the cob, and a salad platter filled wit sliced tomatoes, cucumbers and tender green beans. A spectacular fruit display is accompanied by creamy dip that tastes of summertime. The golden-brown crusted cornbread is Jeannette's own skille variety.

## CRUSTY SKILLET CORNBREAD

| | |
|---|---|
| 2 cups yellow cornmeal | 2 tsp. sugar |
| 1/2 cup flour | 2 tsp. baking powder |
| 1/2 tsp. salt | 1 egg |
| 1/2 tsp. soda | 1 1/4 cups buttermilk |

Mix all of the dry ingredients together. Stir egg into buttermilk and add to the dry mixture. Barely coat inside of a heavy black iron skillet with oil and heat it thoroughly. Pour the cornbread batter into the hot skillet and bake in a 400 degree oven until it has a crispy golden brown crust, about 25 or 30 minutes.

## CREAMY ORANGE FRUIT DIP

1 can condensed milk
8 oz. cool whip
Orange juice

Blend condensed milk and cool whip. Stir in orange juice, adding slowly, until satisfactory consistency is achieved.

## MUSTARD GREENS COOKED with TASSO

Use 3 or 4 bundles of mustard greens. Pick tender parts of leaves away from the ribs. Wash thoroughly more than once. Put 2 tablespoons shortening in large heavy pot and heat well. Add washed greens, but no extra water. Tasso is the Acadian version of jerky. It is very hot and spicy and no extra pepper should be used with it. The best way to use it with vegetables is to cut it into biteable strips and fry it lightly with chopped onions. This seems to bring the flavor out in both. At least 1/2 pound of meat should be used, and if tasso is not available, ham, salt meat, or pickled pork cut in chunks may be added. In South Louisiana, almost all vegetables are cooked with some form of meat. Halfway through cooking the greens, add some Tabasco if you didn't use tasso and want it to be hotter, and cook until everything is tender. Add more water as you cook, if necessary, because the pot liquor is a really important part of this dish and is best absorbed with huge chunks of cornbread. When the meal is finished the empty bowls should be spotless. Kale, chard, turnip tops or any other greens may be cooked in the same manner. Some cooks like to add a light roux to the pot liquor.

## JEANNETTE'S RICE PILAF

| | |
|---|---|
| 1 stick butter | 1/2 tsp. black pepper |
| 3 lg. onions (chopped) | 1 1/2 tsp. paprika |
| 2 cups long grain rice | 1/4 tsp. basil |
| 2 cans chicken broth | 1/4 tsp. thyme |
| 1 tsp. salt | 1 tsp. garlic powder |
| 1/2 tsp. red pepper | 1/2 tsp. dry mustard |

Melt butter over medium heat. Saute onions in butter un tender, stirring occasionally. Add unwashed rice and coc with onion mixture for 20 minutes. Add chicken broth and seasonings. Cook until most of the liquid has disappeare Stir a few times while cooking. Turn to low, cover, and coc until rice is done (approximately 20 minutes). Do not st again!

## FRIED LOUISIANA JUMBO SHRIMP

Peel shrimp, leaving tail and one section of shell. Slic down back (not through), remove vein, and open to form fantail. Season to taste with salt and red pepper.

Batter: 1 cup flour
3 eggs (beaten)
1/4 cup milk
1 box cracker meal

Beat eggs and milk together. Coat shrimp (individually with flour. Dip in egg mixture. Coat generously with cracke meal. Deep fat fry at 350° for about 5 or 6 minutes unti golden brown.

*One of the guest cottages at Tezcuco*

Dining Room at Tezcuco Plantation

# Houmas House
### Burnside, Louisiana

*Houmas Hou*

*Houmas House, its name derived from the Houmas Indians, is undoubtedly one of the finest homes in the United States. It is a monumental structure topped by a windowed belvedere which afforded a view of surrounding Burnside Plantation and the passing river boats. The home was built in 1840 by John Smith Preston on land acquired by his father-in-law, Wade Hampton, a Revolutionary War General. Saving the original four room dwelling at the rear, the Prestons attached it to the great house by an arched carriage way. Garconnieres for the planter's bachelor sons and visiting boys (garçons) were traditional on most creole plantations, but the tall hexagonal ones at Houmas House are ur usual and almost as famous as the house itself. The kitchen (a room in the original dwelling) is one the best in Louisiana, and here the soft cypress table is set for luncheon with old Country-French chin and typically Creole food: oyster and hearts of artichoke soup, French fried crab fingers, crabmeat au gra tin and asparagus salad. The food was prepared by Vince's Restaurant of Donaldsonville.*

*Recipes from Vince Sotile of Vince's Restaurant*

## ASPARAGUS SALAD

Arrange spears of asparagus on a bed of lettuce and accompany with wedges of tomato, hard boiled eggs, black olives and hot peppers. Serve with Vinaigrette Sauce (see page 16 for recipe).

*Garconniere*

## HEARTS OF ARTICHOKE SOUI with OYSTERS

| | |
|---|---|
| 1/4 cup butter | 1/2 can evaporated milk |
| Heart of celery, chopped fine | (or more, if necessary) |
| 2 sweet onions | 1/4 cup parsley, chopped |
| 2 dozen oysters | 1/4 cup green onion tops, choppe |
| 1 can cream of mushroom soup | 2 cans artichoke hearts |
| "All Season" (or seasoning blend) | (chop one can only) |
| to taste | Salt and pepper to taste |

Sauté onions and celery in butter, add oysters and chopped a tichokes from first can and simmer all for a few minutes. Ac mushroom soup and milk. Put chopped parsley and green onio tops in cream mixture and simmer until vegetables are all tende Add whole (or halved) artichoke hearts and heat ten minute longer. Sprinkle All Season over the top just before serving.

## CRAB MEAT au GRATIN

| | |
|---|---|
| 1/2 stick of butter | 1 pound lump crabmeat |
| Inner heart of celery | 2 eggs, well beaten |
| 2 large onions | 1 can evaporated milk (or heavy cream) |
| 1/4 pound Velveeta Cheese, melted | |

Sauté finely chopped celery and onions lightly in butter unt golden. Add lump crabmeat, eggs and evaporated milk, mi lightly, and warm over low heat. Stir continually until well blende and thoroughly heated. Do not overcook. Place in individua ramikins, pour cheese over top and glaze under preheate broiler for a couple of minutes.

## EXCELLENT PIE CRUST
### (See page 8)

| | |
|---|---|
| 2 cups flour | 1/3 cup margarine or butter |
| 1/2 teaspoon salt | 1/3 cup white vegetable shortening |
| | Ice water (about 1/3 cup) |

Mix salt into flour. Work both shortenings into flour with pastry mixer or by crossing two knives against each other. Bits of shor tening should be pea sized. Moisten dough with ice water by stir ring with a fork. Pat into 2 balls (for 2 crusts), wrap in wax paper and chill thoroughly. This dough handles easily and bakes very well. *Author's recipe*

*Kitchen at Houmas House*

# FRENCH FRIED CRAB FINGERS

Crab claws should be "double battered" before frying. Make a batter of egg and a little milk. In a separate bowl mix a teaspoon of baking powder with a cup of flour and mix well with a fork. Season crab fingers with salt, black pepper, red pepper and All Season (or any blend of seasonings). Dip claws in batter, then in flour. Dip in batter again and also in the flour a second time. Deep fry in 325° fat till light brown. Serve with lemon wedges.

# Bocage
## Burnside, Louisiana

*Bocage, meaning a small wood or copse, w* one of the Bringier family homes of which the were many along the river. Marius Pons Bring. had established a grand plantation, White H. (now gone) near Union, La. He built Bocage, a fe miles upriver, for his daughter, Francoise, who h. married Christophe Colombe of Corbeille, Fran. Apparently "Fanny" had learned well from h. father, for she ran the plantation while Christopl wrote poems and songs to his wife, painted p. tures of plantation life, and traveled the river

*Bocage Plantation House*

neighboring plantations in a luxurious little sil canopied barge. The house is a gem of pure classic architecture. The two narro central columns originally flanked a staircase to the second floor parlor. In this se ting, desserts are served on a black marble topped table, along with strong aft dinner coffee and a liqueur. (In earlier days, liqueurs were often concocted by genteel maiden aunt!) Creole coffee, traditionally blended with roasted chicor was always taken in demitasse cups. The desserts, Peaches Lafitte, Orang Snowball Delight, and Chocolate Celeste, were prepared by Lafitte's Landing Donaldsonville.

*Powder House (replica)*

*Recipes of John Folse*

## PEACHES LAFITTE

Serve in parfait glasses.
Spoon vanilla pudding in the bottom of each glass.
Add blue food coloring to Bourbon and pour over pudding.
Sauté peaches in peach brandy and layer above pudding whi hot.
Top with hot whiskey sauce. Serve hot.
Garnish with whipped cream and peach slice.

## CRÊPES SUZETTES
### (See picture on page 35)

| | |
|---|---|
| 4 rounded tablespoons flour | 1 cup milk |
| 1/2 teaspoon sugar | 2 tablespoons cool melted butter |
| 2 eggs | Pinch of salt |

Put flour, 1 egg and egg yolk, salt, sugar and 4 tablespoons milk into a bowl. Beat until quite smooth with a whisk. Then add remainder of milk and cooled, melted butter. Mix in beaten egg white, cover & let stand in refrigerator at least 1/2 hour. Any type of crêpe pan may be used, and after crêpes are browned lightly, they should be stacked on a cake rack. Spread each pancake on one side with some orange butter, made as follows: Cream butter, add some sugar and the grated rind of one orange, and mix in a little Grand Marnier and cognac. Fold the crepes twice into quarter sections or roll up and set aside.

| Sauce: | 3 navel oranges | 6 sugar cubes |
|---|---|---|
| | 3/4 cup granulated sugar | Grand Marnier |
| | 1/2 cup butter or margarine | Cognac |

Put in a chafing dish the butter, sugar, sugar cubes (which have been rubbed on the outside of an orange), the juice and finely grated rind of another orange, the Grand Marnier and cognac.
Simmer gently until rind is translucent, then add skinned sections of one orange and put crepes in to heat gently through. Add more Grand Marnier and cognac if necessary. Warm cognac in a ladle by holding a match under it and then light it. Pour lighted cognac in and flame ingredients in chafing dish thoroughly. (Do not use too much juice or mixture will not flame.) Fresh or canned mandarin or tangerine sections may be used instead of orange sections. Cold liqueur will not ignite well.
*Author's recipe*

## WHISKEY SAUCE:

| | |
|---|---|
| 1 cup sugar | 1/2 stick butter |
| 1 cup heavy cream | 1 well beaten egg |
| | 1/4 cup Bourbon |

Heat butter, sugar and eggs in a heavy pan over low heat. Re move and add Bourbon. Put in blender and run at high speed ti frothy.

## CHOCOLATE CELESTE

Bake your favorite devil's food cake in a square pan or use bakery cake. Place large square of cake on a dessert plate, top with golden vanilla ice cream and pour dark creme de cocoa ove all. Garnish with whipped cream and shaved chocolate.

## ORANGE SNOWBALL DELIGHT

With the hand, quickly roll a hard round scoop of orange sher bert in shredded coconut. Serve in parfait or sherbert glasses. Pour coconut amaretto over ball, cover with whipped cream and place cherry on top. Sprinkle multicolored confetti decorating candies over whipped cream.

*Upstairs Parlor at Bocage*

Dining Room at Hermitage

# Hermitage
## Darrow, Louisiana

*Michel Doradou Bringier, son of Marius, began building his dwelling house in 1812. He had served under Andrew Jackson in the Battle of New Orleans and named his home after Jackson's Hermitage in Tennessee, but gave it the French pronunciation with silent "h", L'Hermitage. The thousand acre plantation which first grew indigo was later planted in sugar cane. The house is the earliest example of Greek revival plantation architecture in Louisiana, and although the exterior presents a grand appearance, it is simple on the inside and reminiscent of Williamsburg homes. Saints' feast days were very important to Creole families. St. Louis, King of France, was a favorite saint of the Bringiers so the Jambon St. Louis (ham) was named for him. One of the typical meals cooked and served to tour groups visiting the plantation is pictured on the dining room table. Shown with the Jambon are herbed rice, glazed yams, marinated green bean salad and pickled okra. Dessert is a Bundt-type lemon cake.*

L'Hermitage

Gazebo (replica)

## JAMBON ST. LOUIS
## (Ham St. Louis)

2 cans cream of mushroom soup
1 cup Chablis
2 cans sliced mushrooms, drained
3 cups cooked ham,
   cut in 1/2 inch cubes
1/4 cup chopped pimento
1 small green pepper, chopped
2 small onions, chopped
2 tablespoons butter

Sauté pepper, onions and ham in butter. Blend soup and Chablis. Add mushrooms and pimento. Heat to boiling point and add ham mixture. Keep hot and serve over herbed rice. (Serves 8). Served with grits, this also makes a delicious dish for a brunch.

## GLAZED YAMS

2 large cans Louisiana Yams (save juice)
2 tablespoons brown sugar
2 teaspoons cinnamon

Place all ingredients into a sauce pan. Cook over a slow fire until liquid thickens to glaze yams. (Serves 6-8).

## FIESTA LEMON CAKE

Mix together 1 package of lemon Jello and 3/4 cups boiling water and set aside to cool.

Mix at medium speed: 1 package yellow cake mix, four eggs (one at a time), 3/4 cup oil and 2 teaspoons lemon extract. Add Jello.

Grease Bundt pan well with margarine or oil. Pour batter into pan and bake for 35 to 40 minutes at 350°. Cake rises above level of pan but will fall. Place plate over cake and invert to remove.

Icing: Use 2 cups of powdered sugar and juice of 2 or 3 lemons. Mix well and spoon over cake while cake is still hot. Garnish with lemon slices, if desired. Any flavor of Jello can be used accompanied by a similar flavor in icing and garnishes.

## MARINATED GREEN BEANS

2 cans cut green beans
1 small jar sliced pimento
1 onion cut in rings
1/2 cup chopped celery

Marinade:
   1 cup oil
   3/4 cup vinegar
   1 teaspoon onion puree
2 tablespoons sugar
2 teaspoons paprika
Salt and pepper to taste

Place all ingredients in a bowl. Cover with marinade. Let stand in refrigerator at least 12 hours or longer before serving. Keeps at least 1 week in refrigerator. (Serves 6-8).

*Recipes from Susan Judice of Hermitage*

## PICKLED ONIONS
### (Picture on page 55)

4 cups sliced sweet onions
2 cups cider vinegar
1/2 cup sugar
4 teaspoons salt
1/2 teaspoon garlic salt
1/4 teaspoon white pepper

Bring mixture to boiling point, drop in onion and turn heat off. Cool and keep in refrigerator. *Author's recipe*

# ottoway Plantation

### White Castle, Louisiana

Viewed from a stern-wheeler, Nottoway is the grandest sight of all, for it is said to be the largest remaining antebellum plantation home in the South. It towers above the landscape and dwarfs all mortal men. Built by John Randolph of Virginia in 1858 and meant to be different from anything built previously in Louisiana, it was designed by the famous architect, Henry Howard. Everything in the magnificent White Ballroom was white — friezes, marble mantles, woodwork, floors. John Andrews, another Virginian, was also building a mansion near White Castle, the designer being

*Nottoway Plantation Hou*

James Gallier, Sr. of New Orleans. Andrews' house, Belle Grove, was by final count the larger for it ha seventy-five rooms and enormous Corinthian columns, but as it no longer exists, Nottoway now hold the title. In spite of the fact that these homes were built by "les Americains" and not by the French, th Creole cooking of the region invariably exerted its influence on the food served to the families. The re taurant at Nottoway prepared the meal for this elegant dining table set with Sevres china. Roast beef wi. creole gravy is accompanied by rice dressing, green beans with sausage, corn with onions and piment tomatoes vinaigrette, pickled beets, and of course, biscuits and cornbread. Babas au Rhum historical served in the French country along the southern banks of the Mississippi, is probably one of the most f. vored desserts. Interestingly, the Creoles referred to the Mississippi banks as coasts (côtes).

## VINAIGRETTE SAUCE

| | |
|---|---|
| 1/3 cup olive oil | 2 tablespoons ketchup |
| 1/3 cup tarragon vinegar | 1 tablespoon chopped parsley |
| 1/3 cup lemon juice | 1 tablespoon basil |
| 2 tablespoons sugar | 1/4 cup sweet pickle relish |
| 1/8 teaspoon dry mustard | 1 chopped hard boiled egg |
| 2 tablespoons chopped pimento | Salt and black or red pepper to taste |

Mix vigorously and warm gently for a few minutes. Refrigerate and use to pour over salad. Tomatoes, asparagus and other vegetables are better when marinated in vinaigrette ahead of time.

*Author's recipes*

*Courtyard garden*

## BABAS au RHUM
### (Baba Cakes in Rum)

| | |
|---|---|
| 1 package yeast | 1/4 cup sugar |
| 1/2 cup warm milk | 3 eggs |
| 2 cups flour | 1/2 teaspoon salt |
| 1/2 stick soft butter | 1 teaspoon vanilla |

Sift flour with salt. Dissolve yeast in warm milk, not hot. Be eggs, add sugar gradually, and whip vigorously until lemon c ored. Melt butter (preferably unsalted) and add to eggs wh warm. Add vanilla and stir in yeast with milk. Beat in enoug sifted flour to make a medium thick batter. You may not need of 2 cups. Let rise in a warm place until double in bulk. Bake buttered, floured muffin tins (about 3/4 full) about 20 minutes until golden in color. If you have fancy shaped molds to bal these in, they look elegant.

Make a simple syrup of sugar and water in a saucepan ar boil. Remove from heat, add 1/4 cup rum, and pour over cak until soaked. Serve with whipped cream or ice cream. Fruit, suc as orange sections or cherries may be added.

*Author's note: Savarin is a large single baba baked in a rir mold. The center is then filled, often with sugared strawberri and some kind of cream.*

## RICE DRESSING

| | |
|---|---|
| 1 pound ground meat | 1 tablespoon basil |
| 3 cups cooked rice | 1 tablespoon thyme |
| 1/2 cup chopped onions | Pinch of cloves and paprika |
| 1/2 cup chopped bell peppers | Dash of Tabasco |
| 1/4 cup chopped parsley | 1 can beef broth as needed |
| 1/4 cup chopped celery | |

Brown ground meat in a little bacon drippings. Add onior peppers, parsley and celery before meat is fully brown, and sau with meat. Turn heat to low simmer, add seasonings and cook rice. Turn quickly and lightly while adding beef broth to blend t gether and moisten. Don't let mixture get mushy.

*Dining Room at Nottoway*

# ROAST with CREOLE GRAVY

Start with roast of your preference at room temperature. Rub surface of roast well with coarsley cracked pepper, sprinkle with salt and pound into roast with heel of hand. Make slits at intervals and press a clove of garlic into each slit. Place roast on rack in an open shallow pan and brush meat with oil or melted butter or baste with Italian salad dressing.

Set oven on broil and leave for 20 minutes. Close oven, set at 400° and continue roasting. A meat thermometer in a finished roast should show 130° for rare, 140° for medium, and 160° for well done. Wait until the thermometer is 5° lower than desired temperature, remove roast from oven, and cover loosely with foil, and leave for 20 minutes.

Meanwhile, make roux with equal amounts of shortening and flour, depending on size of roast and amount of gravy you want. (See page 8 for roux). Add chopped onion, celery, parsley and green onion tops. It is preferable to sauté them first. Squeeze juice out of cloves of garlic, and add pinch of ground cloves, 2 tablespoons basil, salt to taste, Tabasco and paprika. Mushrooms may be included and gravy will taste smoother if a tablespoon of sugar is added.

17

When the paddle wheel boats arrive in Baton Rouge, their passengers debark and visit homes in the city that were originally part of large plantations. They can also take a short excursion on the M.V. Samuel Clemens.

## SPLIT PEA SOUP
(picture on page 21)

| | |
|---|---|
| 1 pound split peas | 1 cup celery, chopped |
| 1/4 pound ham hocks | 1 clove garlic, chopped |
| 1 large onion, chopped | Salt and pepper |
| 6 pints water | |

Saute onion, garlic and celery till wilted. Add to ham hock split peas and water. Simmer over low heat about 2 hours. A water when necessary.

## SHRIMP MOUSSE
(picture on front cover)

| | |
|---|---|
| 1 package of cream cheese (8 oz.) | 2 tablespoons chopped green onions |
| 1 can tomato soup | 2 cups chopped shrimp |
| 2 tablespoons unflavored gelatin | 1/2 teaspoon paprika |
| 1/2 cup water | Salt and pepper |
| 1 cup mayonnaise | Dash Tobasco |
| 2 tablespoons lemon juice | 2 tablespoons horseradish |

Melt cream cheese in hot soup. Blend well. Add slowly to gelatin which has been dissolved in water. Stir all other ingredients into cooled mixture and pour into mold greased with mayonnaise. Refrigerate at least six hours, preferably overnight. Loosen edge gently with knife, cover with serving plate and invert. Garnish with parsley. Made without shrimp (or other seafood) this is a good substitute for tomato aspic, especially with sliced pimento olives and chopped pecans added to it. *Author's recipe.*

 ## SPIDER CORNBREAD
(picture on page 21)

A "spider" (iron pot with three short legs) was placed on t hearth over hot coals to bake this.

| | |
|---|---|
| 1-1/2 cups white cornmeal | 2 eggs, well beaten |
| (preferably water ground) | 2 cups buttermilk |
| 1 teaspoon salt | 1-1/2 tablespoons butter, melted |
| 1 teaspoon baking soda | |

If cooking in an oven, preheat to 450° and put an iron skillet the oven to warm. Sift together cornmeal, salt and baking sod Add the buttermilk to the beaten eggs, then stir into the cornme mixture until smooth. Add melted butter. Pour into the war skillet which has been well greased with bacon drippings. Bake 450° for 30 minutes. (Serves 8)

*Recipes of Kitchen Docents at Magnolia Mound*

# Mount Hope
## Baton Rouge, Louisiana

*Mount Hope*

*Mount Hope, although not grand and pretentious, has great charm and warmth and is said to be the oldest lived-in house in Baton Rouge. When the restoration was completed, authentic replicas of a gazebo and a pigeonniere (dovecote) were constructed on either side of the grounds, in front of the main house. The central hall and flanking rooms, though smaller than those of later and more grandiose plantation homes, have great style and dignity. Mount Hope was built in 1817 by Joseph Sharpe, a German planter of practical nature, and reflects his desire for a sturdy home rather than the architectural showcases of his French contemporaries. The bountiful repast was prepared by Anne Dease, Chatelaine (owner mistress) of Mount Hope, and is typical of those served to group tours. The meal begins with a fruit compote and features Shrimp Creole, probably the most commonly served yet tastiest dish in Southern Louisiana. French-cut green beans, a shrimp mould and homemade braided French bread are served with the entrée. Dessert presents a choice of butter pound cake and banana nut bread.*

*Recipes of Anne Dease of Mount Hope*

## SHRIMP CREOLE
### (see front cover for picture of food)

| | |
|---|---|
| 1/4 cup flour | 5 teaspoons salt |
| 1/4 cup bacon grease | 1 teaspoon pepper |
| 1-1/2 cups chopped onions | 1/2 teaspoon red pepper (optional) |
| 1 cup chopped green onions | Tabasco sauce to taste |
| 1 cup chopped celery with leaves | 2 to 3 bay leaves |
| 1 cup chopped bell pepper | 1 teaspoon sugar |
| 2 cloves garlic, minced | 1 teaspoon Worcestershire sauce |
| 1 six-ounce can tomato paste | 1 tablespoon lemon juice |
| 1-16 oz. can chopped tomatoes with liquid | 4 pounds peeled raw shrimp |
| 1-8 oz. can tomato sauce | 1/2 cup chopped parsley |
| 1 cup water | 2 to 3 cups cooked rice |

Make a dark brown roux of flour and bacon grease in a large heavy pot. (see page 8 for roux directions) Add onions, green onions, celery, bell pepper and garlic and sauté until soft. Add tomato paste and mix this well with vegetables. Add all other ingredients except last three. Simmer slowly for one hour, covered, stirring occasionally. Add shrimp and cook until done, 5 to 15 minutes. This should set awhile and is much better made the day before and reheated but not boiled. Freezes well. Add parsley just before serving. Serve over rice. Serves 10.

*Gazebo (replica)*

## NEW ORLEANS FRENCH BREAD

6-1/2 cups all purpose flour
2-1/4 cups water
4 packages dry yeast
3/4 teaspoons sugar
1-1/2 teaspoons lard
4-1/3 cups all purpose flour
1-1/2 cups water
2-1/2 teaspoons salt
2-1/2 tablespoons sugar
2 tablespoons lard or Crisco

Combine first 5 ingredients in a large mixing bowl; mix with heavy duty electric mixer at high speed for 5 minutes. Place dough in lightly greased large bowl, turning to grease top. Cover dough and let rise in a warm place (85°) free from drafts for 4 hours. Return dough to large mixing bowl. Add remaining ingredients and beat at high speed 10 to 12 minutes. Turn dough into 4 equal portions and shape each portion into a 14 inch loaf. Place loaves on greased baking sheets. Put a pan of boiling water on the lower rack of oven to obtain steam. Bake at 425° for 25 to 30 minutes or until done. Dough may also be braided as shown in one large loaf.

## COCONUT POUND CAKE

1 lb (6 sticks) Kraft's
  Miracle Whipped Margarine
3 cups sugar
3 cups flour
9 eggs
2 teaspoons vanilla
1/2 teaspoon salt
1-1/2 cans Angel Flake coconut

Cream margarine, add sugar slowly, and cream well. Add 4 eggs, one at a time, beating well after each addition. Add the remaining 5 eggs alternately with the flour and salt, beginning and ending with the flour. Add vanilla and mix well. Lastly, fold in the coconut carefully by hand. (Do not use a mixer here, as it will cause the cake to fall slightly.) Pour into a large tube pan and bake in a 325° oven for 1 hour and 45 minutes. Start the cake in a cool oven - do not preheat. An ordinary angel food pan is two small for this cake. Test cake with a toothpick for doneness.

(See page 56 on The Burn for Banana Nut Bread. Anne prefers lemon flavoring to vanilla. See page 18 for Shrimp Mousse).

19

# Magnolia Mound

## Baton Rouge, Louisiana

*Magnolia Mound*

*Magnolia Mound is set on a ridge not far from t* *river and is an authentic early house built in t* *late 1700's. Under the guidance of the Foundatic for Historical Louisiana, with support from t* *Baton Rouge city-parish government, it w* *dramatically saved from destruction in the 196( and faithfully restored to museum quality. The vc unteer "Mound Builders" give tours. A replica of ε early outside kitchen with open fireplace has be* *added and the "Kitchen Docents" (teachers) wt have researched early recipes, have given us demonstration of their cooking. Inside this kitche*

chickens are roasting on a spit in a reflector oven while bread is set near the fire in a long handled ca iron toaster. The table is laden with typical old time foods: split-pea soup, sweet potatoes that have bee roasted in their jackets in a bed of ashes, cornbread, collard greens, jambalaya, crawfish pie and molded blanc mange. A garden salad has been freshly tossed and the cornbread is just ready to con from the oven. An oven has also produced brown sugar pound cake and sponge bread. A sugar mold fε compressing a cone of sugar in the manner of a salt block is shown near the cake.

## CRAWFISH PIE

| | |
|---|---|
| 3 pounds crawfish tails (or shrimp) | 1 bunch parsley, chopped |
| 1/2 cup flour | 1 cup celery, chopped |
| 2 sticks oleo | 1 bell pepper, chopped |
| 1 onion, chopped | 3 tablespoons tomato sauce |
| 2 cloves garlic, chopped | 1 recipe flaky French pastry |
| 2 bunches green onions, chopped | |
| (keep tops separate) | |

Melt oleo, add flour, brown darkly, add garlic, onions, green onion bottoms, bell pepper, celery and tomato sauce. Cover and simmer about one hour, stirring frequently. Add 3 cups water and continue to simmer for several hours. Add more water, if necessary, but mixture should be creamy and thick when tails are added. Cook 15 minutes more until crawfish are tender. If it now gets too thin, add 2 tablespoons of cornstarch creamed with water. Add onion tops and parsley. Pour filling gently into bottom pie shell. Cover with a top crust into which slits have been cut or a lattice top wth strips of dough. Bake at 350° for 15 minutes, then at 300° for 12 to 15 minutes until golden brown. (Serves 6)

## SPONGE BREAD

| | |
|---|---|
| 2 pkg. dry yeast, softened in 1/2 cup warm, not hot, tap water | 5 cups sifted unbleached flour |
| 1/2 cup raw sugar, or light brown sugar, not packed down | 1-1/2 teaspoons salt |
| | 2 tablespoons olive oil |
| 2 cups warm, but not hot tap water | 1-1/2 cups unsifted whole wheat flour |
| (Makes 2 large round loaves) | |

Combine softened yeast, raw sugar, warm water and 2 cups unbleached flour in a large bowl and beat until smooth. Cover with a cloth. Set in a warm spot, let rise about 30 minutes until very light and spongy. Stir in salt and olive oil, then mix in whole wheat flour and 2-1/2 cups unbleached flour. Again cover with a cloth, set in warm spot and let rise until doubled in bulk, about 45 minutes. Turn out on very well floured board (dough will be soft and sticky) and knead in about 1/2 to 3/4 cups unbleached flour until dough is no longer sticky and feels elastic.

Keep hands and board well floured. Knead vigorously about 10 minutes. Divide dough in half, knead each half about 25 to 30 times, then shape into round loaves about 5 inches across. Place in greased layer cake pans, cover with cloth, and let rise until doubled in bulk, about 45 minutes. Bake in 400° oven about 30 minutes until richly browned and hollow sounding when tapped. Remove from pans and cool on racks at least 10 minutes. Cut into wedges and serve.

## CHICKEN and SAUSAGE JAMBALAYA

Bring to a rapid boil 2 quarts water to which the following ha been added:

| | |
|---|---|
| 1 large onion, chopped | 1 tablespoon salt |
| 4 ribs celery, chopped | 1/4 teaspoon Tabasco |
| 1/2 bunch chopped shallots | |

Boil for 10 minutes, then add a medium large chicken ar cook until done. Remove bird, skin and debone. Strain stock ar reserve. Simmer 1 pound smoked sausage in small amount water for 5 minutes. Drain and brown the sausage in a little bu ter. Cut sausage into bite size chunks and set aside. Sauté tr following in butter and fat from sausage:

| | |
|---|---|
| 1 cup finely chopped onion | 1 cup chopped shallots |
| 1/4 cup finely chopped bell pepper | (green onions) |
| 1 cup chopped celery | 1 garlic clove, pressed |

Combine all above ingredients in a large iron or cast aluminu pot, mix well, then add one 1-pound can tomatoes, 2 cups ra rice, 3 cups chicken broth, one tablespoon sugar, salt, cayenr pepper and black pepper as desired. Cook over medium heat, s often but gently until rice is cooked and browned. Serve at onc

## ROAST CHICKENS

Stuff with onion, garlic clove and 1/4 apple. Roast on rack spit in 375° oven. Baste periodically with butter.

*Old recipes researched by Kitchen Docents of Magno Mound*

(Recipes for Greens on p. 43, Blanc Mange and Brown Sug Pound Cake on p. 44, Corn Bread and Pea Soup on p. 18)

*Kitchen (replic*

Kitchen at Magnolia Mound

*Ballroom at Madewood*

## BREAD PUDDING SUPREME

| | |
|---|---|
| 12 slices regular bread | 1 cup granulated sugar |
| 3 cups milk | 1 stick oleomargarine |
| 4 eggs separated | 1 large apple, cored and |
| 1 teaspoon vanilla |    sliced in round slices |

Cream oleo and sugar until light and add egg yolks and vanilla. Add bread which has been soaked in milk and remaining milk and stir well. Grease baking dish. Fill with alternate layers of bread mixture and apples, ending with bread on top. Place casserole in pan of water and bake in 350° oven until knife comes out clean when testing — about 30 to 35 minutes. Remove from oven and add meringue topping made from beating 4 egg whites with 4 tablespoons sugar until peaks form. Brown lightly, in 325° oven. Serve with whiskey sauce (see page 12).

# Madewood
## Napoleonville, Louisiana

*Madewood Plantation House*

*Two fine homes were built on the banks of Bayou Lafourche in Assumption Parish by the brothers Pugh, Thomas and William, from North Carolina. You will note that Louisiana has parishes, not counties. William's house, Woodlawn, no longer exists but Thomas Pugh's house, Madewood (1848), still stands – a splendid sight indeed. The architecture of Madewood is impressive in scale, but simple and pure in style, displaying tall Ionic columns across the front and wings at either side which duplicate features of the central structure. The Pughs were not French, but obviously liked festivities well enough to incorporate a ballroom into Madewood. People in Creole country loved to have soirées, which were evening parties at home – usually involving music and possibly dancing. Tables are set at one end of the Madewood ballroom for a soirée for us, with such favorites as pumpkin, yam and apple casserole served in an enormous shiny pumpkin, tomato and sausage jambalaya, eggplant with ham, and a colorful watermelon fruit basket. Guests at this fête have a choice of bread pudding topped with meringue or juicy plum dumplings. The duck centerpiece is made out of a cushaw pumpkin. Everything was prepared in the Madewood kitchen.*

*Recipes from Naomi Marshall of Madewood*

(See page 20 for Jambalaya recipe.)

## MADEWOOD PUMPKIN LAFOURCHE

6 medium yams or 3 cans, drained
6 medium apples, peeled, cored and sliced
2 cups sugar
1 cup raisins
1 teaspoon vanilla
1 teaspoon cinnamon
1/2 teaspoon nutmeg
1 stick butter or oleo

Peel and cube one medium pumpkin, place in a cast aluminum pot, add a cup of sugar and water to cover. Cook covered at 300° till tender, and cook apples and yams separately with 1/2 cup sugar each, until water has cooked out of all three. Combine in greased baking dish. Cut lid out of nicely shaped, flat bottomed second pumpkin, remove seeds, and grease with cooking oil. Bake at 250° for 30 minutes, but not till too soft. Place on tray and fill with hot mixtures. Replace lid to retain heat till served.

*Creole families spread throughout the French country of South Louisiana and they often took little excursions on smaller boats that could navigate such waterways as Bayou Lafourche and Bayou Teche. Creoles loved to visit their families and sometimes made their stay a lengthy one, so we may want to follow suit.*

*Carriage House at Madewood*

## EGGPLANT - MADEWOOD STYLE

3 cups boiled and drained eggplant
1/2 loaf stale French bread, cut up, and toasted.
3/4 stick butter or margarine
1/2 cup chopped celery
2 cups chopped boiled ham
1/3 cup chopped onions
3/4 cup chopped bell pepper
3 tablespoons finely chopped parsley
1/3 cup vegetable oil
1 teaspoon paprika
1 teaspoon sugar
1 tablespoon Worcestershire sauce
1 teaspoon salt
1/2 teaspoon black pepper
1 teaspoon Accent
Dash Tabasco
2 bay leaves
1/3 cup fine bread crumbs for topping

Sauté onions, bell pepper and celery in oil in a cast aluminum pot. Add ham and heat 10 minutes more. Add eggplant, stir and heat until excess water is gone; then add moistened bread, and all other ingredients. Mix well, fill greased casserole, top with bread crumbs, and place in 375° oven for 30 minutes.

## INGE'S VIENNESE PLUM DUMPLINGS
### (Made especially for Madewood Plantation)

Remove the stone from 3 dozen blue plums and insert a sugar cube in each. Melt one stick of butter in a large pyrex dish. Combine 1 cup sugar, 1 cup bread crumbs and 1 teaspoon cinnamon and spread mixture over bottom of buttered dish. Set aside.

DUMPLING DOUGH: Boil six medium potatoes in their jackets. Cool, peel and put through ricer. Set in oven a few minutes to remove excess moisture. Add approximately 1/2 cup of flour (depending on moisture in potatoes), 1/2 cup Farina or Cream of Wheat, 2 egg yolks, 1 teaspoon salt and 1 tablespoon melted butter and work into a large ball. Have a pot with 2-1/2 quarts boiling water ready. Flour hands, surround each of 12 plums with a thin piece of dough and seal it in tightly. Drop into boiling water, stir gently with wooden spoon to prevent sticking, reduce heat and boil gently until dumplings rise to top.

Cut off fire and let stand for about 3 minutes. Transfer to pyrex dish and put remaining plums around and between dumplings. Cover top with same mixture of sugar, bread crumbs and cinnamon added to stick of melted butter. Bake in 350° oven until bubbly. Serve hot. *Inge O'Quin's recipe*

23

The Shadows

# Shadows on the Teche
## New Iberia, Louisiana

*Sitting atop a bank above Bayou Teche is a tas[t]fully designed rosy pink brick home with the tra[di]tional white columns and dormer windows. Prot[ec]tive green jalousies shelter each end of the up[per] and lower galleries. This is The Shadows, [l] owned by Weeks Hall, a direct descendent of Da[vid] Weeks who built it in 1831. The great-grandson h[as] been called "the last of the Southern gentleme[n]" and he was responsible for the sympathetic resto[ra]tion of this house and for the bequest that left [the] house to The National Trust for Historic Preser[va]tion along with his entire estate to finance its p[er]petual care. Patout's Restaurant in New Iberia has set his table with a game and seafood dinner, typica[l of] this Acadian Country, which surely would have been to his taste. Bowls of Shrimp and Crab Stew p[re]cede Roast Wild Duck and Shrimp and Ham Jambalaya in addition to such savory dishes as Shrimp [Ms.] Ann, Shrimp Remoulade, Stuffed Mushroom Caps and Oysters Alexander.*

*Recipes from Alex Patout of Patout's Restaurant*

## ROAST WILD DUCK

6 ducks — Mallard or Teal
6 strips bacon
5 tablespoons flour with
   salt & pepper
3 tablespoons cooking oil
2 cups water

Chop for gravy: 2 onions, 2 bell
   peppers and 1 rib celery.

Chop for stuffing: 1 onion, 1 bell
   pepper, 1 apple and 1 lemon. Mix
   with 2 tablespoons olive oil

Wash ducks well, season with salt and pepper, and fill cavities with chopped mixture of herbs and olive oil. Sprinkle ducks with flour. Brown in hot oil in black iron pot, remove ducks and pour off excess fat. Return ducks to pot, add remaining chopped herbs for gravy, add water and cover. Roast in 350° oven until ducks begin to break at breastbone. Add additional water if needed to keep ducks moist. Place on serving platter and garnish with orange slices, crab apple and parsley. Serve gravy with rice. (serves 6)

## STUFFED MUSHROOM CAPS

12 large mushroom caps
1 lb. cooked crab meat
1 onion, chopped
1 bell pepper, chopped
1 rib celery, chopped
1 stick butter

1/4 cup lemon juice
2 tablespoons chopped onion tops
2 tablespoons chopped parsley
1 cup bread crumbs
Dash of Worcestershire sauce and Tabasco
Salt & pepper to taste

Sauté herbs in butter until soft. Add crab meat, lemon juice and seasoning and simmer for 10 minutes. Add bread crumbs, onion tops and parsley and cook for about 5 minutes. Stir often so mixture will not stick. Cool dressing, stuff mushroom caps with it, and bake in 350° oven for 7 minutes. This makes a delicious appetizer.

## JAMBALAYA

2 lbs. raw shrimp
1 lb. chopped ham
1 medium eggplant, peeled, boiled
   drained and mashed
2 onions, chopped
1 bell pepper, chopped

1 rib celery, chopped
1 stick butter
1/2 cup chopped green onion tops
1/2 cup chopped parsley
Salt, pepper and Tabasco to taste
3 cups cooked rice

Sauté chopped onions, pepper and celery until soft. Add eggplant, shrimp and ham. Simmer 15 minutes. Add rice, onion tops, parsley and seasonings. Mix well and keep warm until ready to serve. (Serves 8 to 10)

## SHRIMP and CRAB STEW

Use 3 lbs. cleaned raw shrimp and 1 dozen crabs, scald[ed] cleaned and cut in shells. Make a roux with 1 cup oil and 1-1/2 t[o] cups flour and 1 can Rotel tomatoes. When roux is golden bro[wn] add 3 onions, 2 bell peppers and 1 rib celery, all chopped. C[ook] until vegetables are soft.

Boil 6 cups water, add enough roux to make a thick sauce a[nd] season to taste. Simmer one hour. Add shrimp and crabs to sau[ce] bring to boil, lower heat and simmer another half hour. When rea[dy] to serve, add chopped onion tops and parsley. Serve over rice i[n] bowl. (Serves 10)

## SHRIMP MS. ANN

30 large shrimp, peeled and butterflied — keep "shorts"
Season with salt and pepper. Arrange on a baking sheet in ro[ws]
*Make sauce with:*
   2 sticks butter
   1/2 cup lemon juice
       1/2 cup each of onion tops and parsley

   1/4 cup dry Vermouth
   1/4 cup Worcestershire sauce

Simmer first 4 ingredients over low heat for 10 minutes. A[dd] chopped onion tops and parsley to sauce. Pour over shri[mp.] Broil for about 10 minutes until shrimp are cooked. Serve as [an] appetizer or main dish with vegetables. (Serves 4)

(Recipe for Oysters Alexander on page 61)

*Evangeline Oak, nearby on Bayou Tech[e]*

*Dining Room at the Shadows*

Traveling to New Iberia we encounter Bayou Teche, a wide, meandering, slowly flowing bayou that conjures up mental images of weeping willows, spreading oaks and lazy afternoons in lush semi-tropical gardens. Camellias and azaleas thrive and bloom earlier in this protective climate.

Jefferson House

# Live Oak Gard
## Jefferson Island, Louisia

*When we travel west a few short
Iberia we come upon a salt dome
of land that is extremely flat. On th
we discover the Old Joe Jefferson home
home to the actor who made his fortune immor-
talizing the part of Rip Van Winkle in Washington
Irving's play. The house itself has a fairy story look
with all its gingerbread-trimmed galleries, jutting
dormers and little porticoes. Surrounding it, underneath ancient oaks, are beautifully landscaped botanical gardens which literally crown a working
salt mine. J. Lyle Bayless from Kentucky has been
responsible for clearing the land and developing this subtropical feast for the eyes. A garden luncheon
has been set, provided by Jacob's Restaurant in Lafayette, against a background of brilliantly colored
foliage plants. It is a light and delicate repast for a hot summer day, beginning with iced, creamy but
piquante vichysoisse. Seafood crêpes and Escargots de Bourgogne are followed by French lemon pie.*

# ESCARGOTS de BOURGOGNE
### (Snails — Burgundy Style)

Wash snails in running water and place in a sauce pan. Cover
with equal amounts of burgundy wine and consommé. Add
chunks of carrots, onions and shallots and a bouquet garni. (A
bundle of herbs, or herbs tied in cheese cloth, usually including
celery, parsley, thyme and bay leaf or other herbs of your choice).
Season with salt and pepper, simmer 15 minutes and cool in
stock. Place snails in clean shells and seal with Snail Butter a la
Bourguignonne (Burgundian snail butter)

Add the following ingredients to one pound of butter:

| | |
|---|---|
| 6 tablespoons finely chopped shallots | 1 teaspoon basil |
| 2 cloves garlic, pounded into paste | 3 teaspoons salt |
| 2 heaping tablespoons of chopped parsley | 1/4 teaspoon pepper |

Place snails in snail dish, sprinkle with bread crumbs and warm
thoroughly in a hot oven (about 10 minutes). More burgundy
wine can be added when snails are placed in dish. Serve with thin
slice of hot French Bread to soak up extra butter.

# VICHYSOISSE GLACÉE
### (Chilled Potato Soup)

Finely slice 2 medium onions and 4 green onions and sauté in
2 tablespoons butter until soft and slightly golden. Add a quart of
chicken broth and 6 peeled and sliced medium potatoes. Add
salt, white or black pepper as desired, and 2 tablespoon horse-
radish. Bring to a boil and simmer for 35 minutes. Run through
blender until creamy, add 1 cup heavy or whipping cream while
still hot. Chill thoroughly. Serve in bouillon cups and garnish with
chopped parsley and chives.

# FRENCH LEMON PIE

| | |
|---|---|
| 3 eggs | Juice of 2 or 3 lemons, |
| 1 cup sugar | depending on size |
| 1-1/2 cups heavy whipping cream | 9" pie shell |

Beat eggs until frothy and lemon colored. Beat in sugar and
then cream. Stir in lemon juice. Pour into pie shell and bake in a
preheated moderate (375°) oven until top is golden brown.
*Recipe of Mrs. Jacobs of Jacobs Restaurant.*

# SEAFOOD CRÊPES

1/4 cup chopped shallots (green onions)
2 tablespoons chopped parsley (fine)
2 tablespoons chopped chives (fine)
1 tablespoon basil
4 tablespoons butter
3 teaspoons flour
1/2 cup sliced mushrooms
1 dozen or more crêpes
1/2 cup white wine
2 cups or more light cream
2 eggs
1 cup cut up cooked shrimp
1 cup cooked lump crabmeat
Cut up scallops or lobsters may be added
Salt and freshly ground pepper to taste

Sauté chopped vegetables in 2 tablespoons butter until
golden, add flour and simmer 3 more minutes. Add mushrooms,
wine and cream. Simmer until somewhat thickened, about 10
minutes. Cool slightly and add slowly to well beaten eggs. Sauté
all seafood separately in 2 more tablespoons butter and add to
seasoned cream mixture. Use half of the sauce to spoon into the
crêpes, roll up crêpes, and place in baking dish seam side down.
Spoon remaining sauce over the top and bake in oven until well
heated. As a variation, curry powder can be added to this recipe.
Garnish with parsley and paprika.

*Author's recipes*

Garden Scene

*Dining Room at Oaklawn Man...*

# BRIOCHE DOUGH

| | |
|---|---|
| 2 packages dry yeast | 1 teaspoon salt |
| 1/4 cup lukewarm water | 1/2 cup sugar |
| 1 cup milk | 4 eggs, well beaten |
| 2/3 cup butter | 4-1/2 cups sifted flour |

Soften yeast in water. Scald milk, add butter and stir in salt and sugar. Butter will melt. Cool to lukewarm and add yeast and eggs.

Beat in flour, place in large bowl, and let rise in a warm place hours. Chill overnight, then turn out on a floured board. Flatt with palms of hands, roll into a rectangle and cut in half. R each half to 1/8 inch thick. Dough is now ready to make crust f fish. This recipe is enough to cover one large fish or two sm ones, or make rolls with left overs.

# Oaklawn Manor
## Franklin, Louisiana

Oaklawn Manor House

*Massive and monumental" best describes Oak-
~~on~~ Manor which is a virtual fortress with 20-inch
~~wa~~lls and a tremendous foundation. It was built in
~~18~~37 by Alexander Porter, an Irishman who be-
~~ca~~me a statesman representing "Cajun" (Acadian)
~~co~~untry. Such favorite Louisiana trees and shrubs
~~as~~ magnolia, sweet olive, crepe myrtle, cedar and
~~ole~~ander are planted around enchanting gardens
~~an~~d along walkways. This magnificent house has
~~sur~~vived hurricanes, years of neglect, a dangerous
~~fire~~ and the wear of time and weather. Evening
~~su~~pper is set at one end of the long mahogany
~~tab~~le for the Seigneur, lord of the manor. Red Snapper en Croute surrounded by spinach with Bearnaise
~~sa~~uce was created by chef Olivier, and elegantly served on a Bavarian plate. Broccoli and cauliflower are
~~al~~so topped with Bearnaise, while Hare Terrine completes the meal. Note the gold tâte-vin (wine taster)
~~ne~~ar the bottle.*

*Author's recipes*

## RED SNAPPER en CROUTE

~~"F~~ish en Croute is something like Beef Wellington, as it is baked in
~~a c~~rust. The crust can be made of Brioche dough or Puff Paste. The
~~fish~~ may be used whole, deboned, or not boned. This recipe is an
~~ada~~ptation from French haute cuisine that will be easy for all of us
~~ev~~eryday kitchen cooks."

~~B~~uy 2 large filets of Red Snapper or other good size fish, either
~~fre~~sh or frozen. Take some of the loose fish around the edges or
~~bre~~ak up a small filet, and process it with cream and salt and pepper
~~un~~til a little creamy but not too much, to make a mousse. Roll
~~bri~~oche or puff paste dough into two rectangles 1/8 inch thick,
~~m~~aking sure they are larger all around than the largest filet. Place
~~pa~~rchment paper on a cookie sheet, roll up one rectangle of dough
~~on~~ rolling pin and then unroll it onto the parchment. Lay the largest
~~fil~~et on it, spread the mousse over the filet, and sprinkle well with
~~fin~~ely chopped parsley, chives and dill. Lay the second filet on top of
~~the~~ mousse but reverse the large and small ends of the two filets.
~~Sa~~lt and pepper lightly. Beat one egg with one egg yolk for a glaze,
~~an~~d brush the dough around the edge with it. Unroll second layer of
~~do~~ugh over the top and press all around the edge of the fish to seal
~~ed~~ge of dough. Trim un-needed portion away, leaving a small seam
~~aro~~und the fish, making it the shape of a fish and leaving a good

"tail" at the end. Use scraps of dough to fashion eye, mouth, gills
and fins by trimming it with scissors. Put ridges in tail with a fork and
mark a pattern of scales with the top of a teaspoon. Brush with egg
glaze. Bake about 50 minutes in a preheated 350° oven or until
juices just begin to ooze out of the pan.

Serve with the following sauce:

| | |
|---|---|
| 1 cup Sauterne | 2 sticks unsalted butter (or salted) |
| 1/4 cup chopped parsley | 2 egg yolks |
| 1/2 tablespoon chives | 1/2 teaspoon white pepper |
| 1/2 tablespoon tarragon | 1/2 teaspoon salt |

Bring wine to boil and cut heat. Simmer herbs in wine for 1
minute, bring to boil again and turn heat off. Pour in blender
while still hot, add egg yolk, salt, pepper and half a stick of butter.
Blend 1/2 a minute, add remaining butter, and blend for another
half a minute. Do this at the last minute so you can serve it immediately along with the fish. Keep fish warm in a very low oven
'till sauce is ready.

## HARE TERRINE

Step 1:
  This recipe will make 2 terrines. Dice the following meats: Meat
of hare (or substitute domestic rabbit or chicken), 1/2 lb. lean
fresh pork, 1/2 lb. veal, 1/2 lb. fresh pork fat. Season with salt
and lemon pepper and marinate in 1/2 cup of Madeira to which 3
slices of carrot, a bay leaf, thyme, a small onion and a sprig of
parsley have been added. Leave 3 hours.
Step 2:
  Chop the following finely: Meat from back legs, 1/2 lb. of fresh
lean pork and 1/2 lb. of fresh pork fat. Pound all this together in a
mortar and season with a spiced salt mixture. Bind together with
two whole eggs and add 2 oz. of cognac or brandy.
Step 3:
  Remove vegetables from marinade and drain meat. Combine
pounded mixture and diced meats. Line the bottom and sides of
an earthenware terrine or pyrex casserole with slices of bacon.
Pack meat mixture into lined terrine, fold loose ends of bacon
over the top and place more bacon strips over the top where
necessary to cover. Cover dish with foil. Place terrine in a pan half
filled with water and bake 1-1/2 hours in a hot oven. The meat is
done when juices are clear and fat rises to surface. Remove from
oven, remove foil and weight down by placing a brick covered
with foil on top. This will press out air pockets and let fat rise.
Cool, drain off fat, and remove bacon.
  Make a warm aspic by adding 2 envelopes of gelatine to two
cups of stock which has been heated with more herbs and
spices. Add 1/2 cup Madeira, 2 oz. Cognac and a little lemon
juice. Pour over terrine. Refrigerate and slice.

(Recipe for Bearnaise Sauce on page 39)

~~co~~urtyard

29

*Upstairs Living Room at Frances Plantatio*

# Frances Plantation
## Franklin, Louisiana

*It is always heartwarming to see the earlier homes of Louisiana that were fortunate enough to have been preserved. They preceded the Greek revival style, and true to West Indian influence, their large roofs and galleries which kept the house cool were supported by simple, unpretentious columns. Frances Plantation, built in 1820 by George Deharet, is one such house, and is well placed, facing the Old Spanish Trail with the rear overlooking peaceful Bayou Teche. A light luncheon of gourmet fare is laid out on the marble topped serving piece by Peltier's of New Iberia. Mint Juleps in silver julep cups stand ready to awaken our spirits. The centerpiece decorated with creamy yellow roses makes a presentation of chicken breasts with pecan stuffing. The French porcelain compotes hold broccoli drenched with almond sauce; avocado, orange, mushroom and grape salad with bacon dressing; and miniature Grand Marnier tarts. Butter crust bread nestles in bunches of fresh grapes.*

Frances Plantation House

## AVOCADO SALAD

| | |
|---|---|
| 2 or 3 ripe avocados | 2 navel oranges |
| Fresh mushrooms | 1 or 2 bunches of seedless grapes |

Refrigerate all ingredients before starting. Peel, clean and separate sections of oranges. Clean and slice fresh mushrooms. Remove seedless grapes from stems and slice avocados into wedges. Toss lightly. Sprinkle with hot salad dressing.

| Dressing: 3 slices of bacon | 1/4 cup lemon juice |
|---|---|
| 1 teaspoon sugar | Orange peel - grated |

Fry bacon to crisp stage, remove and pat dry. Dissolve sugar into hot grease, add fresh lemon juice and bring to a quick boil. Add orange peel and drizzle over cold salad.

## MINT JULEPS

Use a silver julep cup or a large clear glass and crush a few springs of mint in the bottom with a muddler or spoon. Rub the mint all around the inside of the glass, then throw it away. Now fill the glass with finely cracked ice. *Slowly* pour in a measure of bourbon whiskey, then add about 2 tablespoons of water in which a lump of sugar has been dissolved. *Do not stir.* Place a good spring of mint in the top of the glass.

(Recipe for Broccoli with Lemon-Almond Sauce on page 38)

*Live Oak Trees*

*Recipes from Wayne Peltier of Peltier's for a Catered Affair*

## CHICKEN PARISIENNE

Ten-6 oz. deboned chicken breasts
1 pound ground pork
2 small onions
1 bell pepper
3 celery stalks
Parsley
2 teaspoons allspice
Black and red pepper
Salt to taste
1/2 pint whipping cream
1 cup finely chopped pecans
1 egg
1 tablespoon sweet basil

Process 2 of the 10 chicken breasts in a food mill or grinder and set aside. Finely chop onions, bell pepper, and celery and mix well with pork. Add egg, basil, allspice and season with salt and pepper. Season 8 chicken breasts and pound to thickness of a crêpe, but not to the extent that meat breaks apart. In the center of the breast, thinly layer the forcemeat (pork mixture), then the whipping cream and pecans and then the ground chicken. Begin rolling the breast, making sure that all stuffing is well secured. Place on a baking tin (fold side down) and refrigerate for at least 12 hours. One hour before serving, preheat oven to 350° and bake for 45 minutes or until golden brown.

## GRAND MARNIER TARTS

8 oz. Philadelphia cream cheese
1/4 cup powdered sugar
1/8 cup Grand Marnier
1 to 2 tablespoons grated orange rind

Blend all ingredients in processor. Add some Cool Whip to achieve creamy consistency. Fill bite size tart shells.

Top with Grand Marnier Sauce:

2 squares semi-sweet chocolate
1/4 cup granulated sugar
6 tablespoons water
2 tablespoons butter
1/4 cup Grand Marnier

Heat chocolate squares in water. Melt chocolate and add sugar, stirring continually. Add butter and blend. Add Grand Marnier, bring to quick boil and turn heat off. Pour over tarts, top with cherry, and refrigerate until very cold.

# phodel

ckson, Louisiana

ur voyage upriver to the north of
we come to the Feliciana Parishes
a very English part of Louisiana. Here
pa...rs often debark to a bus and visit various
planta...ons. Just to the south, we visit Asphodel on
a side road leading from the river highway toward
Jackson. Asphodel was built in 1820 by Benjamin
Kendrick who gave it a Greek name referring to the
daffodils and narcissus dear to the hearts of 18th
Century English and French poets, thus marrying
the classic in both name and style of architecture.
The main house and adjoining wings represent a

*Asphodel Plantation Hou...*

facade incorporating simple Doric columns. The architecture seems to hug the hill it rises from and live
in great harmony with the surrounding vines and shrubbery. At the rear of the house is a balcony with
pair of curved staircases leading down to the terrace — the whole adorned with wrought iron railing.
Here on the terrace on a very old cast iron table, a summer tea is set forth by the Asphodel Village In
Cucumber sandwiches, ham biscuits and devilled eggs are followed by bite-sized goodies including litt
Pecan Surprise custard pies, miniature blueberry tarts, watermelon balls and tiny cream puffs filled wi
custard and lemon curd.

## PECAN SURPRISE PIES

Place the following in a blender: 1 cup sugar, 4 eggs, 2 cups
milk, 1/2 cup melted margarine, 1/2 cup flour, 1 teaspoon vanilla and 1 cup chopped pecans or pecan meal. If blender will not
contain the entire mixture, reserve some of the milk to add later.
Pour mixture into miniature pie pans or muffin tins (or into a
10-inch pie pan). Bake 1 hour at 300° or until set. The pie makes
its own crust. Serves 8.

## ⊗ NOOTSIE'S DEVILED EGGS

Add the following ingredients to mashed egg yolks: chopped
green onions, chopped parsley, dry mustard, juice from Kosher
dill pickles, mayonnaise (preferably homemade), salt and freshly
ground white pepper.

## SWEET FILLING for CREAM PUFFS — ASPHODEL STYLE

Make up an instant custard pudding, according to directions
on box. Fold in equal amount of whipped cream. Fill each puff
with 1/2 teaspoon of custard topped with 1/2 teaspoon of lemon
curd. It is better to buy a jar of lemon curd from the gourmet food
department than to try to make it.

*Marcelle Reese Couhig's recipes from Asphodel Village I...*

(Recipe for Ham Biscuits on page 50 and Homemade Mayo
naise on page 56)

## PÂTE a CHOUX

This is a basic cream puff paste that will serve for both desse
filled with sweet creams and appetizers filled with vegetables
meats in a cream sauce for it is unsweetened. Puffs are excelle
with shrimp filling.

| | |
|---|---|
| 1/2 cup butter | 5 eggs divided |
| 1 cup water | 1 cup sifted flour & pinch of salt |

Combine butter, salt and water in a pan and boil till butter
melted. Lower heat and add flour. Beat well and mixture will b
up in center of pan. Cut heat, reserve one egg and beat in
mainder one at a time. Beat dough until velvety smooth a
shiny. Dough may be kept covered in refrigerator for a couple
days. Drop paste on greased baking sheet with small teaspoo
about 2 inches apart. Beat remaining egg with a teaspoon
water and brush tops of miniature cream puffs with a pas
brush. Bake at 425° for 20 minutes or to a golden color. (Lar
puffs bake 10 or 15 minutes longer at 375°). Remove from ove
pierce side of each with knife, and return to oven. Turn off he
and leave door open slightly for 10 minutes more. Cool, sl
tops to make lids, and fill. If you freeze, recrisp in oven befc
filling. Makes 50 small or 25 medium puffs.

## MINIATURE BLUEBERRY TARTS

A variety of high-bush blueberries grows in the Delta a
picking blueberries is considered an outing by the natives. A
flour used in this recipe would be considered shocking
Asphodel.

| | |
|---|---|
| 2 cups blueberries | 1 teaspoon vanilla |
| 1 cup sugar | 1/3 stick of butter |

Mix first 3 ingredients, fill tart shells, and chip butter on top
each. Bake ten minutes at 450°, continue baking and wate
carefully. Time will depend on size of tarts. Filling will be run
when removed from oven, but will thicken as it cools. If this re
ipe is used for a large pie, with a top crust, reduce heat to 35
after initial baking and bake about 30 minutes longer.

*Old Brick Steps in Abandoned Garden, Asphodel*

Oakley Plantation House

# Oakley Plantation
### St. Francisville, Louisiana

*A little farther north, between Asphodel and Francisville, another side road leads to a Louisia State Commemorative Area where we tour house in which John James Audubon taught a stroll through the surrounding woodlands wh he drew many of the birds in his famous Fo Oakley was built by a Scotsman, James Pirrie, 1799, but Audubon was a Frenchman, and cause he tutored the young people he interjecte strong influence into the culture of the area. Th we see the french tastes still following us up Mississippi to some extent. Adding up the visual fect of Oakley's two stories, plus attic and raised brick basement, one is given the impression of a t mendously tall house, though it pre-dates the grand Greek houses. Original Audubon prints ha throughout the house, the Wild Turkey and Blue Heron shown here in the dining room, being two of most coveted in Louisiana. The dinner was prepared by Jacques' Restaurant at the Sheraton in Bat Rouge and displays Chateaubriand set off by fluted creamed potatoes and colorful vegetables. The de blue Staffordshire china holds Louisiana seafood gumbo, spinach salad, Crab Monte Carlo and Crêi Suzettes.*

*Recipes from Chef Charlie Miles of Jacques' at the Sheraton*

## CHATEAUBRIAND BOUQUETIERE

This is a method of preparing a beef filet that was invented by Montmireil, Chef to Chateaubriand. The Chateaubriand should weigh between one and two pounds. It is a thick slice of beef filet taken from the thickest part of the eye of the tenderloin. It is usually grilled, but it can also be sautéed in butter.

To grill, first brush the Chateaubriand with butter or other fat and season. Turn broiler or grill high before putting on filet in order to seal in the juices of the meat. As soon as well seared, lower heat, but inside of meat must be kept rare. Care must be taken that the outside of the meat does not become charred while the inner meat stays raw.

This recipe calls for serving the Chateaubriand with a medley of fresh vegetable in drawn butter and Bordelaise Sauce. (See page 44 for recipe)

## SEAFOOD GUMBO

| | |
|---|---|
| 1/2 cup flour | 2 pounds shrimp |
| 1/2 cup vegetable oil | 1 pound crab meat |
| 1 large onion | 1 quart oysters with oyster water |
| 1 pod garlic | 2 bay leaves |
| 1/2 bell pepper, chopped | 1 tablespoon Worcestershire Sauce |
| 1/4 cup chopped parsley | 2 quarts or more of water |
| Salt, pepper and Tabasco and filé to taste | |

Make a roux by browning 1/2 cup flour in 1/2 cup of well heated vegetable oil. (See page 8 for method.) Add onion, garlic, pepper and parsley and cook 30 minutes. Add crab meat. This can be freshly cleaned crabs or fresh or frozen lump crab meat, but it is nice to have the crab claws and a few chunks from the body of the crab in the gumbo.

At this time, add the bay leaves, Worcestershire Sauce and seasonings, but save filé. Cook 15 minutes. Add the shrimp and oysters and cook about 5 more minutes on a high heat until oysters begin to curl. Do not overcook shrimp and oysters. Cut the heat off, add filé and serve. Filé is powdered sassafras leaves and is a thickener, so don't overdo it. A tablespoonful is about right.

## CRAB MONTE CARLO

| | |
|---|---|
| 1 stick of butter | 2 ounces sherry wine |
| 1/4 cup finely chopped shallots | 4 tablespoons flour |
| 1/2 cup mushrooms, sliced thin | 1 cup cream |
| 1 pound lump crabmeat | 1/4 cup chopped parsley |
| Salt and pepper to taste | 1/4 cup grated cheddar chee |

Sauté shallots and mushrooms in butter until golden. lump crabmeat, salt and pepper and sherry wine. Simmer fo minutes. Add flour to half a cup of cream, beat briskly with a f and add to crabmeat mixture. Heat over low fire until blended thickened. Spoon crab sauce onto 8 crêpes, roll each crêpe place in a shallow baking pan. Add cheese and parsley to ot half cup cream and heat until cheese is melted. Pour over crê and place in a preheated 350° oven for ten minutes of until b bly and lightly browned.

(See page 37 for Spinach Salad and page 12 for Crêpes Suze

*Carriage Hou*

*Dining Room at Oakley*

*Breakfast Room at Rosedou*

# EGGS RAREBIT

4 large eggs at room temperature and 3 English muffins, split and toasted.

*Sauce:*
| | |
|---|---|
| 1/2 stick butter | 1 pound hoop cheese |
| 2 tablespoons margarine | 1/2 cup dry sherry |
| 1/4 cup milk | Dash of Tabasco |
| 2 tablespoons flour | Paprika |

In a shallow saucepan bring water to a boil. Add a teaspoon or two of white vinegar to water. Reduce heat and poach eggs. To make sauce, melt butter and margarine in a shallow pan and ad flour. Cook for 5 minutes on low heat, stirring constantly. Do n allow to brown. Add milk and cook several more minutes. C cheese into chunks and add to white sauce mixture. After chees has completely melted, add sherry slowly, stirring constantly. Se son to taste with several drops of Tabasco and paprika. P poached eggs on muffins and top with sauce. Garnish wit parsley and strips of pimento.

*Rosedown*

# Rosedown
## St. Francisville, Louisiana

*We forge ahead up the main road now following the River and at the crossroads in St. Francisville we come upon one of the most lavishly decorated and completely furnished homes in Louisiana. Another grand alley of oaks leads to the front entrance of Rosedown and on either side thirty acres of gardens are graced with fountains, gazebos and statuary. One of the favorite rooms in the house is the breakfast room furnished with petite chairs, a side board and little fire-light screens to shield the eyes from the bothersome flickering flames. All are painted a soft green and decorated with chinoiserie exotic flowers and birds of paradise. Into this charming setting, the Kitchen Works of Baton Rouge brought an English brunch consisting of poached eggs on English muffins garnished with a rarebit sauce, huge ham steaks with raspberry sauce, fresh fancy cut tomatoes, popovers with orange marmalade and a sinfully rich trifle in a tall silver compote.*

*Recipes from Susan Hymel of The Kitchen Works*

## RASPBERRY SAUCE

oz raspberry jam
/4 cup unsweetened orange juice
tablespoons fresh lemon juice

Lemon (peel strips from 1 lemon)
1 pt. fresh raspberries (or substitute frozen raspberries)

In a saucepan, heat the jam, juices, and lemon strips, just until ixture boils. Lower heat and let simmer 10 to 15 minutes until ixture reduces and thickens. Remove from heat and add fresh spberries. Serve over slices of fresh baked ham.

## POPOVERS

1 cup milk
1 cup flour, sifted
2 tablespoons cool melted butter

2 eggs, beat lightly
Salt to taste
Sugar, if desired

Mix ingredients quickly and lightly. Heat popover pans until sizzling hot and butter well. (Custard cups can be used). Bake half-filled cups in a hot oven (450°) for 20 minutes. Reduce to 375° and bake at least 20 minutes longer. Serve immediately.

## TRIFLE

ne angel food cake cut in three horizontal layers.
ady Fingers

pint fresh raspberries
recipe of your favorite
English custard

1/2 cup sherry or brandy or rum
8 oz. raspberry or red currant preserves
1/2 cup slivered almonds, toasted
1 pint whipping cream, whipped

Put one section of the angel food cake in a large compote. our some of the liquor over it. Spoon preserves on cake and en spread a layer of custard, allowing it to run over edge a little. epeat sequence and top with third portion of the cake with herry poured on it. Stand lady fingers on end, lining the outer m of the cake. They will stick to the custard. Cover top of cake ith whipped cream. Gently place fresh raspberries in the hipped cream. Sprinkle toasted almonds on top. Simple but legant!

## SALADE de SPINACHE ST. GERMAINE
### (See picture on page 34)

Tear off all the tender parts of young, fresh spinach leaves and oss with thin sliced fresh mushrooms, croutons, Parmesan heese and hot bacon chips. It is nice to make a production of his and toss it at the table. Serve with the following creamy ressing:

1/2 cup mayonnaise
2 tablespoons tarragon vinegar
1 tablespoon sugar

1/2 cup sour cream
1 teaspoon dry mustard
Salt and pepper to taste

Combine ingredients and whisk until well blended.
Author's recipe

*Fountain and Gazebo*

37

# The Myrtles
## St. Francisville, Louisiana

*The most inviting feature that strikes us on a fi*
*visit to the Myrtles is the extreme length of the fro*
*gallery. Numerous French doors equipped wi*
*protective tall blinds, or jalousies, open on to t*
*gallery and a row of dormer windows line the ro*
*above. Framing the entire front gallery are railir*
*and supports of lacy cast iron entwined with a c*
*sign of grapevines. Judge Clark Woodruff built th*
*1830 house on a Spanish land grant and comm.*
*sioned intricately detailed woodwork, medallio*
*and friezes, silver doorknobs and handsome ma*
*ble mantels for his home. Various residents of th*

*Rear of the Myrtles showing Galley and Wing*

*home have sworn to a ghostly presence that visits occasionally. The dining roo*
*table, with its patina reflecting an almost golden glow, is set with delicately fl*
*vored light food for a luncheon: stuffed broiled shrimp arranged in a row bordere*
*with rows of fluffy rice and wax beans with tomatoes. Fresh vegetable salad wi*
*toasted sesame seed dressing, green peas and baby carrots, and a yogurt parfa*
*dessert, complete the meal. Food for this menu was produced by chef Har*
*Limberg in Baton Rouge.*

*Garden Statue*

*Recipes by Hans Limberg*

## STUFFED SHRIMP

Use 16 jumbo shrimp — peeled, deveined and butterflied, leaving tails on.

Ingredients for stuffing:

1/4 lb. crabmeat
1/4 lb. raw shrimp
1/4 cup green onions
1/8 cup chopped parsley
2 cloves garlic
2 tablespoons butter
1/2 cup flour
1 cup milk
2 tablespoons sauterne
Juice of one lemon
1/2 tsp. cayenne
1/2 tsp. salt
2 egg yolks

Run shrimp, green onions, parsley and garlic through food chopper until fine. Melt butter in skillet until foam subsides and add shrimp mixture. Cook 4 to 5 minutes, stirring continually, until all liquid has evaporated. Add flour and mix well. Add milk and wine in that order while stirring, and cook over moderate heat until sauce comes to a boil and gets thick and smooth. Add crabmeat and simmer for 2 to 3 minutes. Remove from fire and stir in lemon juice, cayenne, salt and lightly beaten egg yolks. Cool.

Place a small amount of shrimp mixture in each shrimp, close it slightly and place on baking sheet. Salt and pepper shrimp to taste, brush with melted butter, and bake for 3 to 4 minutes (depending on size of shrimp) in 300° oven. While baking, melt one tablespoon of butter with chopped onions and garlic in a small skillet. Place shrimp on a bed of white rice and cover with garlic butter. Accompany this with wax beans and tomato wedges that have been tossed in an herbed butter sauce. Serves 4.

## SESAME SEED DRESSING

This dressing is good for any combination of raw vegetable
The suggested combination here includes tomatoes, cucum
bers, cauliflower, fresh mushrooms, yellow squash and red ca
bage. Vegetables may be parboiled if you prefer.

2 tablespoons honey
1/4 cup wine vinegar
3/4 cup olive oil
3 tablespoons toasted sesame seeds
2 tablespoons chopped green onions
Salt and pepper to taste

Put honey, vinegar and dash of salt and pepper in blender. Sto
blender and add hot toasted sesame seeds and green onions.

## YOGURT PARFAIT

Layer yogurt, fresh berries of your choice, and honey alte
nately until parfait glass is filled. Garnish with a wedge of lime.

## BROCCOLI with
## LEMON-ALMOND SAUCE
(See picture on page 30)

Cut off tough portions and steam broccoli, floret side up, unt
tender. (Do not overcook — keep color bright). Remove an
place in serving dish. Spoon sauce over the top. (A pinch of sod
will help color).

*Sauce:*

| | |
|---|---|
| 1 cup lemon juice concentrate | 1 package sliced almonds |
| 2 sticks unsalted butter | 2 bunches fresh broccoli |

Melt butter, quickly bring to boil, and toss almonds in it. St
once, but watch closely without stirring. Almonds will tend t
soften before regaining their crispness. When almonds brow
quickly pour in lemon juice. Stir quickly but with care, becaus
butter may sizzle and spatter. Immediately spoon over broccoli.
*Recipe from Wayne Peltier*

*ining Room at the Myrtles*

# BEARNAISE SAUCE
### (See picture page 28)

*Author's recipe*

1/4 cup tarragon vinegar
2 chopped green onions
1 tsp. tarragon
4 crushed peppercorns
1/4 cup white wine

3 egg yolks, lightly beaten
1/2 pound melted butter
1/2 teaspon salt
Pinch of cayenne
1 teaspoon chervil

Mix first five ingredients in glass, enamel or porcelain double boiler. Cook over low heat until thick. Mix yolks with one tablespoon water and stir into vinegar mixture. Whip over hot water but do not boil. When creamy, add butter slowly. Stir continually. Add cayenne and salt, strain, and add chervil. Serve immediately.

# The Cottage Plantation

## St. Francisville, Louisiana

*Upriver a little from St. Francisville we dri
down a winding road beneath trees hanging hea
with moss, across a bridge and up a hill to the s
cluded restful world surrounding The Cottage Pla
tation. Here we have the choice of rocking aw
time on either of the lengthy front or back gallerie
A Spanish dwelling built on a land grant in 1795,
was periodically added to by Judge Thomas Butt
between 1811 and 1859, until the present combin
tion was produced. The additions were so w
planned that the pleasing structure seems to ha
been designed all at the same time. Overnig*

The Cottage

guests at the plantation are treated to a healthy breakfast prepared in the kitchen and served on a silv
tray. This particular breakfast, displayed in the front bedroom of the main house, is a specially prepar
gourmet treat sent from Wok "n" Whisk in Baton Rouge. Imagine waking up to spinach quiche, litt
lemon muffins and blueberry muffins, and Estelle's biscuits. Pineapple chunks, cantaloupe balls ar
fresh strawberries garnished with fluffly whipped cream spill out of a pineapple that has been converte
to a cornucopia.

*Recipes from Barbara Peterson of Wok 'n' Whisk.*

## SPINACH QUICHE

Preheat oven to 450°. Note that a large (10-1/2 inch) tart pan with removable bottom (or pie pan) should be used.

*Crust:*

| | |
|---|---|
| 1 cup + 2 tablespoons flour | 3 tablespoons vegetable shortening |
| Pinch of salt | 2 to 5 tablespoons ice cold milk |
| 3 tablespoons firm butter | |

Put flour and salt in a bowl. Gently cut in butter and shortening, using pastry blender or fingers. Work quickly so heat of hands will not "toughen" pastry. Add milk, one tablespoon at a time, until dough goes into a ball. Use least amount of milk for flakiest crust. Roll out between waxed paper. Line pan with dough and prick well with fork. Bake 8 minutes, lined with foil and pie weights (or dry beans) to keep bottom from puffing. Remove from oven and take out foil and weights.

*Filling:*

| | |
|---|---|
| 1 package frozen spinach, defrosted and squeezed dry | 1/4 cup Parmesan cheese, freshly grated |
| 3 green onions, chopped and sautéed in 2 tablespoons butter | 1/4 teaspoon nutmeg |
| 2 eggs & 2 egg yolks | 1/2 teaspoon salt |
| 2 cups Swiss cheese, grated | 1/4 teaspoon white pepper |
| | 1 cup milk |
| 1 cup whipping cream | |

Beat eggs and yolks with whisk, and add cream and seasonings. Sprinkle spinach, onions and grated cheese over prepared shell. Strain custard into pastry shell. Skim off any foam with slotted spoon. Bake at 450° for 15 minutes and at 325° for 20 minutes or until knife inserted in center comes out clean. Remove outer rim from tart pan and let stand a few moments before serving. A quiche can be served with a green salad for lunch or supper, or in small portions or tart shells as a first course.

## PINEAPPLE FRUIT BASKET

Cut top off of a fresh ripe pineapple and reserve for a garnish. Hollow out pineapple, leaving a fairly thin shell. Throw away core and cut remainder up in chunks and add fresh strawberries and melon balls. Arrange fruit as if it were spilling out of pineapple and around the top. Spoon sweetened whipped cream along one side and garnish with parsley. It gives the effect of a cornucopia.

## LEMON MUFFINS

| | |
|---|---|
| 2 tablespoons grated lemon rind | 1/2 cup butter, or unsalted butt |
| 2 tablespoons lemon juice | or margarine |
| 1 cup flour | 1/2 cup sugar |
| 1 teaspoon baking powder | 2 eggs separated |
| 1/4 teaspoon salt | 2 tablespoons sugar |
| 1/4 teaspoon ground cinnamon | |

Preheat oven to 375°. Sift together flour, baking powder a
salt. Cream butter and add sugar, beating until light and flu
Beat egg yolks until lemon colored and add to butter. Add flo
mixture. Do not over mix — just continue until flour disappea
Beat egg whites until stiff. Add grated rind and lemon juice a
fold in egg whites. Fill greased muffin pans 3/4 full. Combine
tablespoons sugar and cinnamon and sprinkle on top of ea
muffin. Bake at 375° for 25 minutes or until done. (Makes o
dozen 2-1/2" muffins, or miniature pans can be used.)

For blueberry muffins, substitute 1 cup blueberries, fres
canned (drained) or frozen in place of lemon rind and juice.

## ESTELLE'S BISCUITS

| | |
|---|---|
| 2-1/2 cups plain flour | 1-1/2 tablespoons baking powder |
| 1/2 teaspoon salt | 3 tablespoons sugar |

Mix flour, salt, sugar and baking powder all together very we
Cut in 3/4 cup Crisco. Add enough milk to hold dough togeth
— about 2/3 cup. Put mixture on floured board, knead a coup
of times, and roll to 3/4" thickness. Cut with a 2" cutter and pla
on ungreased pan. Bake in preheated 450° oven for appro
mately 20 minutes or until golden brown. (Makes 15 biscuit
*Recipe from Estelle Munson, Cottage Cook.*

*Master Bedroom at The Cottage*

*We have progressed upriver to that point not far above St. Francisville where we pass the Mississipp border. Soon we will be in Natchez where busses will again meet the boat and take us to some of th mansions in that fine old city. Perhaps you are a passenger on another boat. Occasionally the Steame Natchez of New Orleans travels upriver to visit its "namesake" city.*

## DEEP DISH APPLE PIE

(See picture on back cover)          *Author's recip*

| | |
|---|---|
| 6 tart apples | 1 tablespoon butter or margarine |
| 2/3 cup sugar | Cinnamon, nutmeg and lemon juice |
| 1 tablespoon flour | as you like it and a pinch of salt |

Use a deep, large pie pan or baking dish and 1/2 again normal pie crust pastry recipe. Wash, pare and core apples. Cut in lengthwise slices. Sprinkle spices and lemon juice over apples. Mix apples, sugar and flour and put all in pie pan lined with your favorite pastry. (or see page 10 for recipe)

Dot top with bits of butter. Cover with a top crust. Make 2 or 3 slits in top crust or use a pie bird to vent steam. Bake 10 minutes at 425° and 30 minutes or more at 350°. Serve with wedges of cheddar cheese.

## HOME MADE PUMPERNICKEL BREAD

(See picture on page 48)

| | |
|---|---|
| 1-1/2 cups water | 1 tablespoon caraway seeds |
| 3/4 cups corn meal | 2 cups mashed potatoes |
| 1-1/2 cups boiling water | 1 envelope yeast (dissolved in a little warm water) |
| 1 tablespoon salt | |
| 2 tablespoons sugar | 4 cups rye flour, mixed with |
| 2 tablespoons oil | 4-1/4 cups white flour |

Stir water into corn meal, add boiling water, cook and stir for 3 minutes. Add salt, sugar, oil, and seeds. Cool until mixture is lukewarm. Add potatoes and yeast. Work in both flours, knead dough well and smooth on a board "floured" with meal. Place dough in greased bowl, grease top and let it double in size. Knead once more and divide into 3 buttered loaf pans. Let rise again until bulk has doubled. Bake in 425° oven for 15 minutes and then lower heat to 350°. Continue baking for 50 minutes. *Recipe from Bobbye J. Porter and Florence Turpin of The Post House*

## SWEET POTATO CASSEROLE

Boil 4 sweet potatoes until tender, peel and mash. Add 1/2 c butter and mash into potatoes. Add one or two eggs and be into potatoes vigorously. Then add 1/2 cup hot milk, 1/2 c brown sugar and a teaspoon vanilla. If you wish, miniatu marshmallows and chopped pecans may be mixed in. Place in casserole, cover top with pineapple rings and cherries, and spri kle brown sugar over top. Bake 20 minutes at 375°.

## SMOTHERED OKRA and TOMATOES

(See picture on page 46)

| | |
|---|---|
| 3 tablespoons cooking oil | 2 tablespoons lemon juice |
| 2 pounds fresh okra, sliced | 1 tablespoon sugar |
| 1 large onion, chopped | 1 or 2 tablespoons |
| 1 can tomatoes, or cut up | Worcestershire sauce |
| fresh tomatoes in | Pinch of ground cloves |
| equivalent amount | Salt & Pepper to taste |

Heat cooking oil in a heavy pot, lower heat and add sliced okr You will need to stir this faithfully, scraping the bottom of the pa all the time, as the gelatinous okra wants to stick. However, you labor will reward you. The seeds will turn pink when it has cooke enough and it will be well smothered down and no longer slim At this point, add the onions and tomatoes and cook down unt very little liquid remains. Add the seasonings as you cook an mash the tomatoes well. The finished product has such a soli consistency and flavor that it almost becomes a substitute fo meat and is very filling. *Author's recipe*

semont

# Rosemont
## Woodville, Mississippi

*Jefferson Davis was such a hero to the Confederacy that every place he ever lived has become a sort of shrine. Rosemont was his boyhood home and you can imagine him walking the paths and climbing the split rail fences that surround this charming house or playing on the back gallery that overlooks a wooded ravine. We thought that what we would most enjoy here would be a real old-fashioned country supper, so sure enough, Rosemont served up one in their quaint old kitchen building just down the walk from the house. It has everything a country kitchen should have from the*
ast iron wood stove to the faded old blue china on the "red-checkered" table cloth. Gigantic thick mothered pork chops are topped with fried apple rings and sweet potato casserole is decorated with neapple slices and cherries. Cornbread and Hopping John with blackeyed peas and ham hocks in a big ack pot can be seen on the stove. Turnip greens are seasoned with salt pork, tomatoes are presented ith cucumbers and zucchini and deep-dish apple pie is served with chunks of cheddar cheese. A cream avy has been made for the pork chops and now we know we are in the country of the Americans of nglish lineage for we have left behind the roux-based dark gravies of the French people.*

*Author's recipes*

## SMOTHERED PORK CHOPS and FRIED APPLE RINGS

Season pork chops well with salt and freshly ground pepper on th sides. Brown quickly in hot fat, pour off excess grease and serve. Add a little water, cover tightly and simmer till tender. ld more water as necessary. Mississippians make a cream avy with equal portions of pork grease and flour, blended but t browned, and gradually add cream or milk. Season with salt d pepper. Brown bits left in the pan and the liquid from the ops should be added to the gravy. Heat until flour is well oked.

Apple Rings: Use firm, tart apples. Core and cut into half inch ck rings. Do not peel. Heat butter or bacon fat in a heavy frying n. Arrange apples one layer thick, brown and turn. Sprinkle th brown sugar (or white) and let melt while second side is owning. Remove with spatula and serve on pork chops.

## HOPPING JOHN

| | |
|---|---|
| 1 pound black eyed peas | 1/4 cup chopped parsley |
| Ham Hocks | 2 bay leaves |
| 1 large onion, chopped | Salt and cayenne pepper to taste |
| 1/4 cup green onion tops | 1/4 cup butter |
| 1/4 cup chopped bell peppers | 2 cups rice |

Wash peas, change water and bring to a rolling boil for a few inutes. Remove from heat and soak overnight in that same ater, enough to cover the peas. In the morning, bring to boil ain and add everything except butter and rice. Reduce heat d simmer for 3 hours. Peas should be creamy but remain hole. Add butter and mix well.

Put rice in 4 quarts boiling salted water to which a tablespoon oil and one of vinegar have been added. Reduce heat some d cook 18 minutes. Drain and rinse in colander. Return colan- er to rest over the pot which has had a little water put in it. eam a few minutes until warmed through. Mix peas and rice d serve with ham hocks.

Serve this on New Years day to bring prosperity throughout the ar. Serve cabbage also on this day and you will have money ming in all year.

## TURNIP GREENS and SALT PORK
### (Served with Corn Bread)

Brown salt pork in an iron or cast aluminum pot and reserve. Strip tender parts of turnip greens from stems and stringy veins, wash thoroughly and wilt down in some grease from the pork, in the same pot. (About 3 bunches of turnip greens should do.) You should not need salt, but add cayenne pepper and 1/2 cup chopped onions. Flavor with 1 tablespoon vinegar and 1 table- spoon sugar. Peel turnip bottoms, cut in cubes, and add to pot. To make the pot liquor even better, add a light roux to the pot about half way through the cooking time. They should simmer for about an hour in the covered pot. If you want them really hot, add some Tabasco.

The main reason for serving cornbread with greens is that all red blooded southerners "sop up the pot liquor" with it, even in polite society. More delicate people crumble it into the liquor left in the bottom of the dish and spoon it up. (See page 18 for cornbread recipe).

(See back cover for pictures of food)

Kitchen

# Auburn
## Natchez, Mississippi

*Aubu...*

*...p the Mississippi as up a spiral stair-... ...g grander sights as we mount higher a... ...r to the north. It is impossible to visit all the ho...es in Louisiana and Mississippi and particularly in Natchez, but we are having a taste of many of the great ones. This free-standing staircase climbs gracefully to the second floor with no visible supporting columns. The ladies at Auburn boast of it and rightfully so! Auburn, an 1812 house, is in the heart of beautiful Duncan Park and now belongs to the City of Natchez. It was a gift from the heirs of Dr. Stephen Duncan, the last owner, and is operated as a historical preservation project by the Town and Country Garden Club. A tea table filled wit... goodies for a late afternoon interlude has been set for us at the foot of the stairs. The titillating dishes, ca... tered from Confederate House include a hot seafood dip in a chafing dish with toast baskets to be fille... cheese tiropetes, and whole strawberries.*

*Recipes from Loveta Byrne of The Burn*

## TIROPETES

Tiropetes are marvelous little hors d'ouvres invented by the Greeks. They are made of fillo dough and you will need about 1/2 pound of it. The Greeks call it "fila" and fold it into triangles. You can fill it with Philadelphia Cream Cheese and do it in a hurry, or you can make your own creamy filling by using 1/2 pound of cream cheese and 1/2 pound of either cottage cheese or ricotta.

Stir 3 eggs into the cheese and season with chopped parsley and black pepper. Cut foot long pieces of fillo into 3-inch strips and brush with melted butter. Put a walnut sized mound of filling at one end and fold to make a triangle. Continue folding triangularly from side to side to either end, exactly as one folds a flag. Brush tops of finished triangles with more butter and bake in medium oven until golden brown. Tiropetes may be frozen and reheated later.

## HOT SEAFOOD DIP

| | |
|---|---|
| 2 tablespoons butter or oleo | 1/2 cup mushrooms, sliced |
| 2 tablespoons flour | 1/2 cup chopped parsley |
| 1 cup or more scalded milk | 1 teaspoon tarragon |
| 1/2 pound shrimp, cut in half | Dash of nutmeg |
| 1/2 pound scallops | Salt and pepper to taste |

Melt butter over low heat, cream flour into it, and add scalded milk slowly, letting it thicken. If it begins to thicken too rapidly while adding milk, remove from fire for a minute. Add milk to desired thinness. Combine seafood, mushrooms and seasoning with sauce and heat until shrimp and scallops are cooked. Serve in toast cases.

Butter thin slices of bread which have been trimmed. Press into muffin tins and toast in moderate oven until browned. If small cases are desired, quarter slices of bread and press into miniature tins.

## BROWN SUGAR POUND CAK[
(See page 21 for picture)

| | |
|---|---|
| 3 cups sifted all purpose flour | 1 cup sugar |
| 1/2 teaspoon baking powder | 5 large eggs |
| 1/4 teaspoon salt | 1 cup milk |
| 3/4 cup butter, at room temperature | 1-1/2 teaspoons vanilla |
| 3/4 cup vegetable shortening | 1 cup chopped pecans or waln... |
| 1 pound light brown sugar | |

Sift together flour, baking powder, and salt and set asi... Cream butter and vegetable shortening until light, add bro... sugar gradually, creaming all the while until fluffy, then add ... plain sugar the same way and cream until very light. Beat in eg... one at a time. Add sifted ingredients alternately with milk, beg... ning and ending with dry ingredients and beating after each a... dition only enough to blend. Stir in vanilla and nuts. Pour into w... greased and floured 10-inch tube pan and bake at 325° for 1-3... to 2 hours or until cake begins to pull from sides and top sprin... back slowly when pressed with finger. Cool cake upright in its p... on wire rack 10 minutes, then invert and turn out on wire rack. ... cool to room temperature before cutting. *Recipe from An... Dease*

## BLANC MANGE
(See page 21 for picture)

| | |
|---|---|
| 1/2 cup blanched almonds | 1/4 cup water |
| 1/2 cup sugar | 1 egg |
| 2 cups milk | 1/8 teaspoon almond extract |
| 1 cup light cream | 1/8 teaspoon vanilla extract |
| 2 tablespoons plain gelatin | |

Process or blend almonds, add to 2 cups milk and gelatin so... ened in 1/4 cup water. Heat to a simmer, process or blend o... egg and sugar, pour hot milk over as you stir. Stir to dissol... sugar. Strain and discard ground almonds. Cool, then add e... tracts. Pour into a 4 cup mold that has been sprayed with Pa... Chill overnight. Invert onto a serving plate. Serve with a fr... sauce to which a little brandy has been added. *Recipe fro... Kitchen Docents at Magnolia Mound*

## BORDELAISE SAUCE
(See page 35 for picture)

| | |
|---|---|
| 2 tablespoons butter | 2 minced green onions |
| 1/8 teaspoon freshly ground pepper | 1 tablespoon minced carrot |
| 2 tablespoons flour | 1 sprig parsley |
| 1 cup beef stock | 1 bay leaf |
| 2 teaspoons Worcestershire sauce | Pinch of ground cloves and salt to taste |

Melt butter in saucepan and heat until just starting to brow... Stir in pepper and flour and simmer until light brown. Add be... stock slowly, stirring all the while and boil gently for one minut... Add all other ingredients and cook 15 minutes, adding mo... liquid if sauce gets too thick. Remove from heat and strain. Ma... be used with Chateaubriand or other meats. *Author's recipe*

*Dairy House*

Entrance Hall at Auburn

*Dining Room at Stanton H*

# Stanton Hall
## Natchez, Mississippi

anton Hall

*Standing majestically at the top of a hill in the center of Natchez, Stanton Hall is truly the Grande Dame of Mississippi homes. Built by a wealthy Irishman, Frederick Stanton, in 1857, it was, as he quaintly put it, an "ornament for the town." One of the most outstanding examples of craftsmanship in the house are the ornate chandeliers which include vining leaves, ears of corn, Indians, horses and many, many other flora, fauna and folk motifs lifted from Natchez history. Today, it serves as headquarters for the Pilgrimage Garden Club and for the annual Pilgrimage in March, when all of Natchez shares her heritage with "pilgrims" from the four corners of the earth. The table in the grand dining room is set with a portion of an extensive set of Vieux Paris china and an array of food which is served daily at the Carriage House on the grounds. An enormous baked ham with brown sugar and honey glaze and a platter of Mississippi fried chicken with brown gravy are offered with choices of tomato aspic, congealed carrot and pineapple salad, yellow squash with pimento, smothered okra and tomatoes, parsleyed steamed rice, tiny biscuits with wild plum jelly, corn sticks, lemon tarts and chocolate tarts.*

## CONGEALED CARROT and PINEAPPLE SALAD

| | |
|---|---|
| 1 package lemon jello | 1 cup finely chopped carrots |
| 1-1/2 cups liquid | 1 cup drained crushed pineapple |
| 2 tablespoons lemon juice | Salt to taste |

Save juice from drained pineapple. Add enough water to make up 1-1/2 cups liquid. Dissolve jello in boiling liquid. Add lemon juice, carrots, pineapple and salt. Pour into individual molds and refrigerate. When starting to thicken, stir carrots and pineapple down in. When set, unmold and serve on lettuce with a dollop of mayonnaise.

## LEMON TARTS

| | |
|---|---|
| 1 cup sugar | 1/2 cup lemon juice |
| 1/3 cup flour | 3 egg yolks, beaten |
| 1/4 teaspoons salt | 1 teaspoon grated lemon rind |
| 1-1/2 cups water | 2 tablespoons butter |

Mix sugar, flour and salt with water in a saucepan. Cook over low heat, stirring constantly, until thickened. Cook another ten minutes until clear, still stirring. Stir 1/2 cup of the hot mixture slowly into the egg yolks, then stir egg yolks into the rest of the mixture in the saucepan. Cook and stir for a few more minutes. Remove and add rind, lemon juice and butter. Cool 15 minutes and pour into prebaked tart shells. Top with a spoonful of whipped cream when serving.

## CHOCOLATE TARTS

| | |
|---|---|
| 3/4 cup sugar | 3 cups milk |
| 1/2 cup flour | 3 egg yolks |
| 1/4 teaspoon salt | 2 tablespoons butter |
| 2 ounces unsweetened chocolate | 1 teaspoon vanilla |

Combine sugar, flour and salt in a saucepan. Melt chocolate in milk in another pan. Stir chocolate mixture into sugar and flour and cook over a low heat until thick, stirring constantly. Add a little of the hot mixture to yolks, then add yolks to saucepan. Cook and stir for 3 more minutes. Remove from fire and blend in butter and vanilla. Cool 15 minutes and pour into prebaked tart shells. Serve with a spoonful of whipped cream.

## MISSISSIPPI FRIED CHICKEN with BROWN GRAVY

Cut up fryer into pieces of desired size. Sprinkle liberally with salt and lemon pepper. Add 1/2 teaspoon each of salt and pepper to one cup of flour in a paper bag. The true secret of taste is to give the seasoning time to take effect, so place the covered chicken pieces in the refrigerator for a couple of hours or more. Cook in a deep fat fryer in oil or lard at 375°. Remove when golden brown and watch closely as small pieces will be ready earlier.

Some cooks like to add 1 teaspoon of baking powder to the flour mixture.

*Gravy:*

| | |
|---|---|
| 2 tablespoons fat (can be rendered chicken fat or oil) | |
| 2 tablespoons flour | Salt to taste |
| 1-1/2 cups chicken stock | Freshly ground pepper |

Heat oil gently and stir in flour. Stir continually and cook for several minutes. It should not be allowed to get lumpy. Add hot liquid slowly, still stirring, until desired consistency is reached. This type of brown gravy is not cooked as intensely as a typical French roux, so it will not be as dark. Other seasoning may be added, if you wish. Sage is nice with chicken.

*Detail of Front*

47

*Dining Room at Longwo[...]*

# BOULA-BOULA SOUP

To one can of green turtle soup, add one can of green pea soup, canned or fresh crabmeat, and sherry wine. Season with 1/4 teaspoon each of basil, marjoram, rosemary, and thyme. Add salt and pepper to taste, and a pinch of ground cloves and anise. Add 1/2 pint of heavy cream or whipping cream and blend gently. Simmer on low heat until thoroughly warmed. Garni[...] with thin rings of red onions. *Cooked by The Post Hou[...] Author's version*

# Longwood
## Natchez, Mississippi

"Nutt's Folly" as it has always been nicknamed, the handsome Longwood that should be called Nutt's Unfinished Masterpiece." Dr. Haller Nutt, a wealthy cotton planter, dreamed this fashionable product of the mid-nineteenth century Oriental style into reality, and commissioned architect Samual Sloan to build it. At the same time that the Northern craftsmen had just begun work on the second level, Fort Sumter was fired upon. The remainder of the house has never been worked on since the day they fled for home. The ground floor, which was intended for working and recreation

Longwood

rooms, was later furnished as a home. The Post House Restaurant, which furnished this grand dinner, is housed in King's Tavern, reputedly the oldest tavern in the Natchez Territory. Both Longwood and King's Tavern are properties of the Pilgrimage Garden Club. Spread before us, underneath a suspended punkah, the Boula-Boula Soup (in the soup plates), prime rib, broccoli and rice casserole, homemade pumpernickel bread, a fruit plate with poppy seed dressing and a cherry cheesecake. In earlier times, a small servant boy sat in the corner pulling a rope from the punkah, thus stirring the air and shooing the flies.

Recipes from Bobbye J. Porter and Florence Turpin of The Post House

(Recipe for Pumpernickel Bread on page 42)

## CHEESE CAKE

Mix the following ingredients together: 1/2 stick of butter (at room temperature). 1/4 cup sugar and 1-1/2 cups graham cracker crumbs. Press mixture on the bottom and fourth of the way up on the sides of a spring form pan.

Filling:
1-1/2 pounds Philadelphia Cream Cheese (at room temperature)
1 cup sugar     4 eggs     2 teaspoons vanilla

Beat cream cheese well, add sugar and beat thoroughly. Add eggs one at a time, beating extremely well after each. Add vanilla flavoring. Pour mixture gently into graham cracker crust. Bake at 375° for 25 to 30 minutes, cool for 5 minutes and spread on a topping made of 1-1/2 cups sour cream mixed with 2 table-spoons sugar and 1 tablespoon vanilla flavoring. Bake at 400° for 5 minutes. Refrigerate overnight or at least six hours before serving. Garnish with cherry or other fruit sauce.

## POPPY SEED DRESSING

1/2 cup sugar
1 teaspoon dry mustard
1 teaspoon paprika
5 tablespoons vinegar
5 tablespoons tarragon vinegar
1/4 teaspoon salt
1/3 cup honey
1 tablespoon lemon juice
2 tablespoons onion juice or
   2 tablespoons finely grated onion
1 cup vegetable oil
1 tablespoon poppy seed

Mix together the sugar, mustard, paprika, salt and vinegars until sugar dissolves completely. Add the honey, lemon juice and onion juice. Gradually beat in the oil. Chill and add poppy seeds when ready to serve.

## PRIME RIB

Let the roast stand for an hour at room temperature before roasting. Rub outside well with salt (1/2 teaspoon per pound of meat) and freshly ground pepper. Place the roast on a rack with the fat side up, or tie suet or bacon on top if it is too lean. Roast in a 325° oven and allow 20 minutes per pound for rare meat, 25 minutes for medium and 30 minutes or more for well-done meat. Pour off fat, save some for gravy and add water to roasting pan to dissolve brown bits of dried juices in order to add them to the gravy.

## BROCCOLI-RICE CASSEROLE

2-1/2 pounds frozen broccoli
2 cups long grain rice
1 cup fresh mushrooms (chopped fine)
1-1/2 medium size onions (chopped fine)
1 cup flour
1 to 1-1/2 cups chicken stock
3 cups whipping cream
2 cups bread crumbs

Boil 2 cups rice 18 minutes, drain and save rice water. Add just enough chicken stock to flavor it, and gently boil the broccoli in the rice water until barely tender.

Sauce: Sauté the mushrooms and onions in butter. Add chicken stock to taste, add flour, and stir well. Then add whipping cream. Add salt and pepper to taste and blend well.

Pour rice in bottom of a large casserole dish, layer broccoli over it. Spread onions and mushrooms over the top, sprinkle bread crumbs over all, and dot with melted butter. Bake at 350° for 20 to 30 minutes. (Serves 6 to 8)

Entrance to Longwood

# Connelly's Tavern

### Natchez, Mississippi

*Connelly's Tav...*

*Connelly's Tavern, a property of the Natchez Garden Club, overlooks the Mississippi from a high bluff. Long flights of stairs lead up Ellicott Hill to this very early (1795) house where tourists can savor the combination of true simplicity and great beauty. Though originally built for a home it later was converted to a tavern by Pat Connelly and his wife, who raised drawbridges at the rear before dark to keep out marauders and varmints. During the year, the ladies of the Preservation Society of Ellicott Hill give small "affairs" for groups such as the Antique Dealers Group that participates in their show or the Crew of the Delta Queen. The fare here is typical of the food they serve. Spread on an o... hutch table are such delights as coffee punch, chicken salad sandwiches with almonds and curry, ha... biscuits in a pewter biscuit box, pralines, blackberry jam cake and grapefruit baskets filled with fre... strawberries.*

*Recipes from Connelly's Tavern*

## BISCUITS SUPREME

| | |
|---|---|
| 2 cups sifted flour | 2 teaspoons sugar |
| 4 teaspoons baking powder | 1/2 cup shortening |
| 1/2 teaspoon salt | 2/3 cup milk |
| 1/2 teaspoon cream of tartar | |

Sift dry ingredients. Cut in shortening. Add milk and mix gently for half a minute. Pat and roll to desired thickness. Cut small biscuits and bake on ungreased cookie sheet at 450° for 10 to 12 minutes.

For party ham biscuits, brush tops with melted butter, and sprinkle with coarse black pepper. Butter and fill with ham before baking.

## BLACKBERRY JAM CAKE

| | |
|---|---|
| 8 ounces sweet unsalted butter | 1 teaspoon freshly grated nutme... |
| 2 cups granulated sugar | 1 teaspoon mace |
| 1 cup buttermilk | 1/4 teaspoon powdered cloves |
| 1 teaspoon baking soda | 1/2 teaspoon powdered allspice |
| 4 eggs, separated | 1 teaspoon vanilla extract |
| 3 cups sifted all-purpose flour | 1 cup seedless blackberry jam |
| 1-1/2 teaspoons cinnamon | |

Preheat oven to 300°. Butter large tube pan and dust lig... with fine dry breadcrumbs. Sift together the flour, cinnam... nutmeg, mace, cloves and allspice. Set aside. Cream the butte... a large bowl with electric mixer, then add vanilla extract. Grad... ally add the sugar, beating for one or two minutes. Add egg yo... one at a time, beating well after each addition. Dissolve the so... in the buttermilk. On lowest speed, alternately add the dry ing... dients in three additions with the buttermilk in two additio... beating only until smooth. Add the jam. Beat egg white in a sep... rate bowl until stiff but not dry. Fold in half the egg whites into ... batter with a spatula, then fold in remaining egg whites and p... into cake pan. Rotate the pan briskly to level the top. Bake 15 m... nutes at 300°, 15 at 350° and 25 to 30 at 360°. If top browns t... rapidly, cover last 15 minutes with aluminum foil. Let cake c... 15 minutes in pan on a rack.

## REE'S COFFEE PUNCH FOR FIFTY

| | |
|---|---|
| 1 cup instant coffee | 5 quarts of frozen Coffee Rich |
| 1 cup boiling water | 4 large bottles gingerale |
| 1 cup sugar | Vanilla ice cream |

Mix together coffee, water and sugar. To this cooled mixtu... add Coffee Rich that has thawed to ice crystal stage. To 1-1... quarts of above mixture add 1 bottle of gingerale. Place in... punch bowl and add 1/3 to 1/2 of a gallon of vanilla ice cream

## PRALINES, THE PARSONAGE STYLE

Bring following mixture to a boil in a very large saucepan:

| | |
|---|---|
| 2 cups white sugar | 2/3 cup boiling water |
| 3/4 cup Pet milk | 1/3 cup white Karo syrup |

Add 1/2 teaspoon soda, bring to boil again, and add 2 cu... pecans. Stir constantly, continuing to firm ball stage. Remo... from heat, and beat until it thickens and loses shiny gloss. Dro... by spoonfuls onto wax paper. Add teaspoon hot water if it b... comes too hard. May be frozen or kept in an air tight container

*Drawbridge*

*Kitchen at Connelly's Tavern*

# CURRIED CHICKEN-ALMOND SALAD

1 cup diced cooked chicken
1/2 cup finely chopped celery
2 tablespoons chopped green onions
2 tablespoons chopped parsley

Mayonnaise as needed
1 teaspoon curry powder
1/4 cup finely chopped almonds
Salt and pepper to taste

Mix all ingredients. Add mayonnaise as needed as you mix, but don't overdo it and kill the flavor. As variations, chopped hard boiled egg or chopped apples may be added.

Meadow and Gazebo at Rosali

# Rosalie
## Natchez, Mississippi

*At the side of Rosalie lies a peaceful green meadow which is the top surface of a river bluff standing above the old brick merchants' buildings that comprise "Natchez-Under-the-Hill". The meadow is surrounded by a split rail fence and large shade trees, and inside this idyllic setting stands a charming wrought iron gazebo. Rosalie, a handsome house of soft red brick and white columns, is the property of the Mississippi Society of the Daughter's of the American Revolution and they maintain it with loving care. Peter Little built the home in 1820 for his young wife Eliza, who,*

Rosalie

*when orphaned had become his ward. The Cock of the Walk, a restaurant down at the end of Natchez-Under-the-Hill, sent up their fried catfish picnic and served it in front of the gazebo. No one fries catfish better than people who live along the great river and the tasty side dishes are true "country cookin'." Amazingly, french fried dill pickles take their place with fried onion rings and french fries; cole slaw in a crockery jar and pickled onions; hush puppies and jalapeno cornbread; plus tartar sauce, mustard greens with fat back and hot gingerbread served with a lemon and honey sauce.*

Author's recipes

## FRIED DILL PICKLES

| | |
|---|---|
| Sliced dill pickles | 1 tablespoon Lea & Perrin |
| Salt | 5 or 6 drops of Tabasco sauce |
| Pepper | 1 tablespoon flour |
| 1 egg | 2 cups flour |
| 8 oz. milk | |

Mix beaten egg with milk, Lea and Perrin, Tabasco and 1 tablespoon flour. Salt and pepper to taste. Mix 2 cups flour with salt and pepper to taste in a separate bowl. Dip pickle in egg wash, then into flour, then into egg wash and back into flour, then into 350° deep fat. Fry to golden brown. *Recipe from Cock of the Walk*

## TARTAR SAUCE

| | |
|---|---|
| 1 cup mayonnaise | 1 tablespoon chopped dill pickle |
| 1 teaspoon onion juice | 1 tablespoon chopped parsley |
| 1 tablespoon capers | 1 tablespoon chopped chives |
| | 1 tablespoon lemon juice |

Stir well and store in refrigerator.

(Recipe for Pickled Onions on page 15 and for Molasses Gingerbread on page 56)

## FRIED CATFISH

Filet catfish. Rinse filets quickly and wipe thoroughly. Add salt and pepper to fine corn meal. Dip fish filets in milk and then in cornmeal. Pop into deep hot fat and fry until golden but don't overfry. Put brown paper on a platter, lay fish on it to drain, and place in a very low oven to keep warm. Cooking oil should be at 375°. The country way is to float a match on the oil and when it lights, the oil is ready for frying. It seems dangerous. I always expect the grease to flame up, too, but it never seems to.

## HUSH PUPPIES

| | |
|---|---|
| 1 cup yellow cornmeal | 1 egg |
| 2 teaspoons baking powder | 1/4 cup milk |
| 1/2 teaspoon salt | Cayenne (red) pepper to taste |
| 1 medium onion, finely chopped | |

Mix together the dry ingredients, including the onion. Break the egg into the meal and beat very well. Add milk, stir, and form into small balls. Drop into deep hot fat, preferably the same one the fish has just been fried in.

## FRIED ONION RINGS

| | |
|---|---|
| 4 large Bermuda onions | 1/2 cup flour |
| 2 cups milk | Salt and pepper |

Cut onions in 1/4 inch slices and separate slices into rings. Soak onion rings in milk first for about a half an hour, stirring about occasionally. Add seasoning to flour, and drop rings in flour a few at a time, turning with a fork until well coated. Fry in hot oil at 370° until golden, but not too many at a time. Drain on brown paper and hold in a warming oven until all are fixed.

## CREAMY COLE SLAW

Slice or chop one head of cabbage as finely as possible. Mix equal amounts of vinegar and sugar and pour in enough to saturate cabbage well. Let stand for several hours, or preferably overnight in the refrigerator. Add mayonnaise and milk or buttermilk. Season with mustard, salt, pepper and poppyseed in quantities to suit your particular taste. Very finely chopped bell pepper is a nice addition to this salad. Letting the cabbage marinate in the vinegar and sugar before adding the other ingredients makes a tremendous difference in the final taste.

Bronze Bell

# Monmouth
## Natchez, Mississippi

*Monmouth*

*Built in 1818, Monmouth is most famous for* second owner, General John A. Quitman, who *the charge on Chapultepec in the War with Mex and raised the Stars and Stripes over the Mexic capital. Monmouth is a massive house that tow at the peak of a hill. The interior has been restore its original elegance and the banquet table shir with beautiful Sevres china, silver candelabra, epergnes and lacy napkins in footed silver nap rings that are animal figures. The Hearth Restaur at the Ramada Inn has great experience behind i preparing traditional Natchez foods. A juicy ve*

*son roast is served upon a silver platter. Venison needs the companionship of su hearty dishes as cole slaw made with green and red cabbage, pickled red a white onion rings, corn pudding, a casserole of turnips au gratin, cross cut yar and grapenut custard pudding.*

*Courtyard*

*Recipes from Clarence Eyrich at the Ramada Inn*

## VENISON ROAST

A haunch of venison is roasted much the same as beef is roasted, only not so long, and moister with a whole cup of water. It is usually allowed to hang in a cool dry place for some time, when fres killed. It is roasted until rare (20 minutes to the pound), medium (25 minutes to the pound), or well de (30 minutes to the pound) in a moderate 350° oven. It may be served with pan gravy and garnished w mint, watercress or parsley. Possibilities for a sauce to accompany venison include raw cranberry reli currant jelly, currant mint sauce, or wild grape jelly such as muscadine. Currant mint sauce is made stirring 1 tablespoon chopped mint leaves and the grated rind of half an orange into a 6 ounce glass currant jelly.

(Recipe for Pickled Onions on p. 15)

## CORN PUDDING

| | |
|---|---|
| 4 cups cut corn | 1 cup milk |
| 4 eggs | 1 stick butter |
| 1 tablespoon pimento — diced | Salt, pepper and paprika |
| 2 tablespoons diced bell pepper | |

Cut corn from fresh cob and then scrape and catch "milk" until you have four cups of corn and liquid. Canned cream style corn or whole kernal corn, or a combination of the two may be substituted. Beat eggs with a fork and add to corn with pimento and bell pepper. Pour in milk, add salt and pepper and mix thoroughly. Spread 1/3 of this mixture in the bottom of a casserole. Dot with pats of butter. Repeat with two more layers of the same. After the butter has been added to the top layer, sprinkle generously with paprika. Bake at 350° until firm.

## CANDIED CROSS-CUT YAMS

| | |
|---|---|
| 4 boiled sweet potatoes (firm) | 1/2 cup sugar |
| 1/4 cup butter or margarine | 1/2 cup water |
| 2 slices of lemon | Red food coloring |

Peel and slice yams crosswise, about 1/4 inch thick. Cook butter, water, lemons and sugar for about 3 minutes, and add red food coloring. Put sliced yams in a baking dish and pour the syrup over them. Bake in a moderate oven (350°) for about 30 minutes. Spoon the syrup over the yams two or three times during the baking. The food coloring makes the orange yams look especially bright.

## TURNIPS au GRATIN

| | |
|---|---|
| 1-1/2 pounds turnips, pared and sliced | 3 tablespoons flour |
| (end product about 4 cups) | 1 cup milk or cream (or more |
| 3 tablespoons butter or margarine | 1/2 cup of sharp cheddar che |
| 1/4 cup chopped onion | (grated) |
| 1/4 cup chopped green pepper | Snipped parsley |
| 1/4 cup chopped celery | Paprika |
| Salt and pepper to taste | |

Cook turnips in enough water to cover, salted and boiling, ur tender. Drain. Melt butter and sauté vegetables until golde Blend flour in slowly, smoothing it in with the butter as you add Add milk as you need it, to the desired consistency. Add chee and salt and pepper, cook on low heat until melted into sauc Combine cheese sauce and turnips and pour into a baking di or casserole of one quart capacity. Top with seasoned bre crumbs or not, as you prefer. Dust top with paprika and sprink with parsley bits.

## GRAPENUT CUSTARD PUDDING

| | |
|---|---|
| 9 oz. sugar | 2 tablespoons vanilla |
| 1/2 cup grapenuts | 6 whole eggs, unbeaten |
| 1/4 cup melted butter | 12 oz. milk |
| 8 oz. grapenut flakes | 1/4 teaspoon salt |

Mix all of the above ingredients together. Pour into a well bu tered baking dish and bake one hour in a moderate oven (350 or until a knife inserted in the center will come out clean.

Formal Dining Room at Monmouth

# The Burn
### Natchez, Mississippi

The Burn, built in 1832, is said to be the earliest Greek Revival house in the Natchez area. The unusual name of John Walworth's home is a Scottish word meaning brook and just such a little brook trickled through his vast estate. As in many Natchez homes, priceless antiques made by such famous cabinet makers as Belter and Mallard are to be found here. You must observe carefully to realize that this gracious dining room on the ground floor is actually somewhat informal, for the grand formal dining room is on the upper level of the house. A small palm in an old jardiniere helps create the atmosphere of a past era. Overnight guests are treated to a sumptuous plantation breakfast prepared i the kitchen near this accessible ground floor room. They have created for us eggs baked in cream wit swiss cheese and bacon and served in tiny silver ramekins, marvelous Orange Blossom muffins, banan bread and a large fruit bowl.

The Bu

Recipes of Bobbie Harper, formerly of The Burn

## ORANGE BLOSSOM MUFFINS

| | |
|---|---|
| 1 slightly beaten egg | 1/2 cup chopped pecans |
| 1/4 cup sugar | 1/2 cup sugar |
| 1/2 cup orange juice | 1/2 teaspoon cinnamon |
| 2 tablespoons salad oil | 1-1/2 tablespoons flour |
| 2 cups packaged biscuit mix | 1/4 teaspoon nutmeg |
| 1/2 cup orange marmalade | 1 tablespoon margarine |

Combine first four ingredients, add biscuit mix and beat for 30 seconds. Stir in marmalade and pecans. Grease muffin pans and fill 2/3 full. Combine sugar, flour, cinnamon and nutmeg, cut in margarine till crumbly, and sprinkle over batter. Bake at 350° for about 20 minutes.

## SWISS BAKED EGGS

Cook slice of bacon until crisp, drain. Crumble bacon in ram kin and add 1 tablespoon cream and 1 tablespoon crumbl swiss cheese. Break egg into ramekin and sprinkle with salt. S ramekin in shallow baking pan filled with water and bake in sl 325° oven for 15 minutes. Sprinkle with 1/2 teaspoon chives a 1 tablespoon cheese. Bake until eggs are set, about 5 minutes longer.

## BANANA NUT BREAD

| | |
|---|---|
| 1 stick butter | 1 teaspoon baking soda and dash of sa |
| 1 cup sugar | 3 ripe bananas whipped well in blender |
| 2 eggs | 1/2 teaspoon vanilla |
| 2 cups sifted cake flour | 1/2 cup finely chopped pecans |

Cream butter and sugar well, add eggs, flour, soda and sa and mix well. Then add bananas, vanilla and nuts. Bake in bread pan, 9-1/2 x 5-1/2 x 2-1/2 lined with wax paper at 350° about 1 hour or until done.

## MOLASSES GINGERBREAD
### (See picture on page 52)

| | |
|---|---|
| 1/4 cup shortening | 1/2 teaspoon salt |
| 1 cup molasses | 1 tablespoon ginger |
| 1 tablespoon vinegar | 1 teaspoon cinnamon |
| 1 egg, well beaten | 1 cup buttermilk |
| 1 teaspoon soda | 2 cups flour |

Melt shortening, add molasses, vinegar and egg. Mix and s dry ingredients and add alternately with the milk. Preheat oven 365°. Grease and flour pan, pour in batter, and bake 30 to 4 minutes. Serve with hot honey and lemon sauce. *Author's recip*

## EXCELLENT HOMEMADE MAYONNAISE
### (Goes with recipes on page 32)

This is used in the cucumber sandwiches and finely choppe parsley has been added to it. Use 2 egg yolks, 1 tablespoon cide vinegar, 1 scant teaspoon dry mustard and 1/2 teaspoon sa Beat until very well blended. Dribble salad oil, a few drops at time, beating constantly on medium speed until it sets up. The continue adding somewhere between 1 to 1-1/2 cups. Consis tency will depend on type of oil used and thickness you prefe Add a teaspoon or 2 of lemon juice. Finally add 1 or 2 teaspoon of boiling water to take away the oily look. *Recipe from Marcell Reese Couhig of Asphodel*

*Formal Garden*

Informal Dining Room at the Burn

McRaven

# McRaven
## Vicksburg, Mississippi

*Not only are we on a trip up the Mississippi, b[ ] we are also on a trip going back in time. Touri[ ] McRaven we travel through three distinct perio[ ] in time in the short distance from the back of t[ ] house to the front door. The oldest back secti[ ] was a typical frontier cottage built in 1825 at t[ ] time Vicksburg was founded and belonged to t[ ] original Newitt Vick plantation. In 1836 Sher[ ] Stephen Howard bought the property and add[ ] the middle section in Greek Revival architecture.[ ] 1849, new owner John Bobb added a Philadelph[ ] Townhouse as the third section in "high" Gre[ ] Revival complete with elegant gas chandeliers. The dining room is in the middle section and we look [ ] the steps and through the door into the last, most cultivated addition. We come upon a virtual paradox [ ] the red paddlewheel pushes us up the River in our "Cookin' on the Mississippi" travels. The farther nor[ ] we go, the more southern the "cookin" seems to get, for North Louisiana and Mississippi folk are mo[ ] rigidly traditional than those inhabitants of South Louisiana and Mississippi, especially the Creoles, wh[ ] live in a more carefree and relaxed atmosphere. The Veranda dining room at the Magnolia Motel has pr[ ] vided us with a casserole of Oysters "Johnny Reb", tomato aspic with carrot curls, garden vegetables [ ] broccoli, cauliflower and carrots in a cream butter sauce, bran muffins, and Down in Dixie Bourbon P[ ] The aperitif is Peaches Mule.*

*Recipes of Restaurant Manager, Rubye L. Jones*

## OYSTERS "JOHNNY REB"

| | |
|---|---|
| 2 quarts oysters drained | 1 tablespoon Worcestershire sauce |
| 1/2 cup finely chopped parsley | 2 tablespoons lemon juice |
| 1/2 cup chopped green onions | 1/2 cup melted butter or oleo |
| Tabasco sauce | 3/4 cup cream |

Place a layer of oysters in a greased shallow baking dish. Sprinkle half of the parsley, onions, seasoning, lemon juice, butter and crumbs. Repeat layer of oysters and seasoning, omitting crumbs. Pour cream evenly over dish. Cover with crumbs and dust generously with paprika. Bake at 375° for 30 minutes or until firm. Serves 12 people.

## DOWN IN DIXIE BOURBON PIE

| | |
|---|---|
| 2 doz. marshmallows | 1/4 cup Bourbon |
| 1 cup evaporated milk | 1 box chocolate snaps or wafers |
| 1/2 pint whipping cream | 1/2 cup melted butter or margarine |

Melt marshmallows in milk in a double boiler but do not boil. Chill. Whip cream and fold into mixture. Add bourbon, pour into cooled chocolate crumb crust and refrigerate until set. Top with whipped cream and chocolate crumbs.

CRUST: Crush chocolate snaps or wafers, mix with butter and pat into 9-inch pie pan. Bake until set and cool.

## TOMATO ASPIC

| | |
|---|---|
| 2 envelopes gelatin | 1 teaspoon Worcestershire sauce |
| 4 cups tomato juice | 1 teaspoon salt |
| 1 small onion, sliced | 1/2 teaspoon pepper or dash of Tabas[ ] |
| 2 ribs celery, chopped | 1 tablespoon sugar |
| 1/4 cup chopped parsley | 1/2 cup water |
| 4 tablespoons lemon juice | 8 oz. Philadelphia cream cheese |

Add everything except gelatin, lemon juice and water to toma[ ] juice. Bring to a quick boil, simmer ten minutes, and strain. D[ ] solve gelatin in water, add to tomato juice and stir well. Wh[ ] liquid clears, add lemon juice. Pour in six individual molds a[ ] drop a spoonful of cream cheese in each mold, or pour in ri[ ] mold and serve with cream cheese in center. Chill until fir[ ] *Author's recipe*

## PEACHES MULE

This house specialty at the Veranda derives its name from [ ] kick. Use a jigger of rum, gin, vodka, Southern Comfort, a[ ] brandy. Add some lime juice for flavor, grenadine for color, and [ ] splash of 7-Up for effervescence. Shake vigorously with ic[ ] strain, and serve garnished with a peach slice. *Recipe fro[ ] Magnolia Lounge*

## SHRIMP with REMOULADE SAUCE
### (See picture on page 25)

| | |
|---|---|
| 1 cup olive oil | 3 jars (5-1/2 oz.) Zatarain mustard (dark, hot) |
| 1 cup Wesson oil | 7-1/2 oz. horseradish |
| 3 cups celery, chopped | 3 tablespoons mayonnaise |
| 3/4 cup vinegar | 10 tablespoons paprika |
| 3 cups parsley | 1-1/2 teaspoons black pepper |
| 1 cup green onion | 1-1/2 teaspoons salt |
| 1-1/2 cups grated onion | 4 dashes Tabasco |

Mix all ingredients together well. This may be bottled and kept in refrigerator until wanted. Use this sauce to pour over boiled, peeled shrimp. Coat shrimp generously with sauce and serve on shredded lettuce or in a bowl with picks as an appetizer. *Recipe from Alex Patout*

*Greek Revival Priv[ ]*

*Dining Room at McRaven*

*Up the Mississippi from Natchez stands another fine old city, Vicksburg, famous for its historic homes of great dignity and charm and also for the grandly designed Vicksburg National Military Park that spreads over the high bluffs above the Mississippi River. There one can leisurely ponder the huge bronze statues commemorating the men from all the states that fought in "The War Between the States".*

*Nursery at Cedar Grove*

# MUSTARD BAKED HAM

Score smoked ham diagonally and stud diamonds with whole cloves. Make a paste with prepared mustard and brown sugar, moistened with Coca Cola and pineapple juice. Add a little cinnamon and ginger. Coat ham thoroughly and bake at least 30 minutes to heat through. Add more glaze during baking.

# Cedar Grove
Vicksburg, Mississippi

Cedar Grove

The last home we are visiting, Cedar Grove (an [?]0 house) has a small room well worth waiting [?] truly a pièce-de-resistance! This pinkest nursery [?] boasts tiny twin Mallard beds with canopies [?]led half testers, but the focal point of the camera [?] being the food, we could only show one. Soft [?]k drapes the bay window and upholsters the lit-[?] settee and chairs making an exquisitely charm-[?] haven for children. More pink bands the French [?]ina enticing little toddlers to the table. [?]minello's Restaurant has a traditional associa-[?]n with Cedar Grove since it is only a block away, [?]d the owner furnished a gourmet supper tailored to children's appetites. Ham with a baked on mustard [?]ce was served with Spaghetti al Burro — a "white" pasta, but first an antipasto platter fit to tempt any [?]ld! Dessert is a tantalizingly colorful Italian fruit parfait served with "coffee-milk" for the tots. And so, [?]king over our shoulder one last time, we close the door and wistfully make our way back to the River [?]our senses saturated with the past, and the food, and the creative people who perpetuate this wonderful [?]rld out of yesterday.

[?]cipes from Michael Berry

## ANTIPASTO PLATTER

[?]erve fresh tomato wedges, halves of hard boiled eggs, crinkle [?] carrots and carrot sticks, blanched cauliflower florets, chilled [?]led shrimp, radish flowers, and half sections of Italian sausage [?] a platter of dark green lettuce or other greens. Place a cup of [?]tipasto dressing in the center.

[?]ressing: Chop 6 black olives, 1/2 onion, 1/4 green pepper [?]d 1 clove garlic. Add to 1 pint olive oil with salt, pepper and [?]sil and a dash of ketchup, and let stand for several hours. May [?] served as is or strained. For a creamy dip, add mayonnaise.

## SPAGHETTI al BURRO
### (A white pasta with a butter cream sauce)

Cook one package of spaghetti or spaghettini in boiling water until tender. Drain well and rinse. Sauté noodles in one stick of butter. Add white wine and simmer a few minutes. Add 1 cup of whipping cream, 1/2 cup or more grated Parmesan cheese to thicken, and more butter as desired. Season with salt, white pepper and a dash of nutmeg. Serve hot and sprinkle with chopped parsley.

## ITALIAN FRUIT PARFAIT

Serve rich vanilla ice cream in coupette or widely flared sherbet glasses. Marinate strawberries, raspberries or mixed fruit in Amaretto liqueur and spoon around ice cream in flare of glass. Top with whipped cream and a piece of whatever fruit is used.

## OYSTERS ALEXANDER
### (See picture on page 25)

(See picture on page 25)

| | |
|---|---|
| 2 onions, chopped | 1/2 pound butter |
| 1 bell pepper, chopped | 1/2 cup chopped parsley |
| 1 cup celery, chopped | 1/2 cup chopped green onions |
| 1 pod garlic | 1 tablespoon lemon juice |
| 1 whole loaf French bread | 1 teaspoon thyme |
| (1/2 soaked in oyster juice and | 6 drops Tabasco |
| 1/2 made into bread crumbs) | Salt and pepper to taste |
| 1 cup Parmesan cheese | 4 pints oysters — 2 pints chopped for |
| 1/4 cup paprika | dressing and 2 pints to put in shells |
| 1/4 cup bread crumbs | 2 pounds shrimp — |
| 1 pint oyster juice | cooked and chopped |

Preheat oven to 450°. Melt butter, add chopped ingredients of onions, bell pepper, celery and garlic. Sauté until soft. Add diced shrimp and oyster juice and cook 7 minutes. (cut oyster just back of eye of muscle — *important*). Add oysters and cook only 4 minutes. Add soaked half loaf of French bread, parsley, green onions, lemon juice, thyme and other seasonings. Cook 10 minutes, remove from heat, and cool. Dressing should be stiff, but will give off juice while oysters are baking.

Place one oyster on each of 2 dozen cleaned oyster shells. Sprinkle with salt and pepper. With your hand, cover each oyster with cooled dressing, thinly, but completely. Place shells on baking sheet. Sprinkle all shells lightly with a mixture of one cup bread crumbs, paprika and Parmesan cheese. Brown in broiler until golden. (about 18 minutes). *Recipe from Alex Patout*

[?]rra-cotta Statue

61

*Buffet lunch served aboard the Steamer Natchez featuring platters of sliced turkey, ham and roast be with tomato wedges, accompanied by 3-bean salad, pickled beets with onion rings and corn relish. De sert is a bowl of ambrosia topped with generous amounts of coconut and cherries. Buffet prepared b Charles Stratton.*

ddlewheeler on the Mississippi

The paddlewheelers are truly the grand ladies of the river. They are admired and onored, they keep a wonderful tradition alive, and they also perpetuate a great link vith our past history. The interior architecture decorating many of these steam ships, ast and present, was as grand as the stately homes they traveled to along the river. We alute this era in American history.

ng's Tavern,
atchez, Mississippi.

Natchez Under-the-Hill,
Natchez, Mississippi

Lafitte's Landing,
Donaldsville, Louisiana

Many of the restaurants along the Mississippi are housed in historic buildings. The hree above are typical and we urge you to search a variety of these out in your travels hrough Mississippi and Louisiana. You will also discover many fine modern rest- urants that serve traditional local foods.

**About the Author:** Bobby Potts lived at Tezcuco Plantation on the Old River Road near Burnside, La. or 30 years. All the neighboring plantation owners visited back and forth, comparing recipes, ympathizing with each other on the various problems of maintaining historic houses, and sharing the oys of having the good fortune to dwell in graceful homes. She writes with great understanding and from ersonal experience of their customs and pleasures, both in present and historic times, and with apprecia- on of the fine foods that the Delta land produced. Cookin' on the Mississippi was a way of life, and the ove of cooking and eating showed itself in the conversations that occurred at every gathering. Hopefully, hrough the pictures and recipes in this book, the reader has vicariously experienced some of the pleasures f living in such a culture.

# Index